6-6-78

About the Book

Author Vernon Pizer in this book takes you on a delightful exploration of the many strange ways people communicate without uttering a word. Humans have made life difficult for themselves by developing more than 5,000 languages and dialects that often bar their understanding a neighbor only a few miles away. In the Soviet Union alone, Pizer points out, nearly 150 languages are spoken and only about half the Soviet citizens understand Russian.

Here are recounted people's efforts—funny, sad, heroic—to communicate with others. Everything from chirps and whistles to smoke and drum signals have been tried. Today a new science of gestural communication called pasimology says that your face and body can create 700,000 different expressions and gestures to tell another what you think without your saying a word. In this book, too, you discover the wonders of and arguments over pictographs and glyphs. On almost every page it offers believe-it-or-not truths about our living together.

YOU DON'T SAY

How people communicate without speech

Vernon Pizer

illustrated by Janet McCaffery

G. P. Putnam's Sons · New York

Copyright © 1978 by Vernon Pizer
All rights reserved. Published
simultaneously in Canada by
Longman Canada Limited, Toronto.
PRINTED IN THE UNITED STATES OF AMERICA

Library of Congress Cataloging in Publication Data
Pizer, Vernon, 1918-
You don't say.
Includes index.
SUMMARY: Recounts the efforts of people to
communicate without words, using such means as the
voice, music, color, gestures, pictographs and
glyphs.
1.   Nonverbal communication—Juvenile literature.
2.   Signs and symbols—Juvenile literature.
[1.   Nonverbal communication.   2.   Signs and
symbols]   I.   Title.
P99.5.P5   001.56   77-12576
ISBN 0-399-20625-6

Contents

YOU DON'T SAY

1

The Trail From Babel

• A novice motorist, venturing alone on her first long-distance drive, passed a roadside sign reading: "Merge Right." While she was still trying to interpret the cryptic meaning of the sign, she rounded a curve and slammed into the steel drums marking the end of her lane.

• Alarmed by a flurry of reports of children being burned because their fire-retardant pajamas ignited, the U.S. Commission on Consumer Products launched a thorough investigation. The Commission determined to its satisfaction that the manufacturer had properly processed the fabric to render it resistant to fire. But it also discovered that the laundering instructions on the label were so complicated that many mothers, confused by them, were unwittingly washing the protection out of the garments.

• A midwest firm ordered an expensive, complex piece of machinery from abroad. It arrived intact and undamaged but was nevertheless unusable because every one of its dials, knobs, and switches was marked in German.

• Prescribing medication for an ailing patient, a doctor clearly instructed her to take two capsules three times daily at mealtimes. At the end of a week the patient's condition had become worse. The problem was that to the doctor "mealtime" meant at the *start* of the meal while to the patient it meant at the *end*. To have any healing effect, the medicine prescribed had to be absorbed into the body with food, not after it.

• One of the giant U.S. oil companies, trying to boost sales of its gasoline, sought a new brand name with more punch than the old one. In the nick of time, it learned that one name under serious consideration was identical to that of a German poison gas used for genocide in Nazi extermination camps while a second leading candidate was identical to the Japanese word for a stalled car.

• Villagers in a famine-stricken area of Asia welcomed a relief shipment. After a number fell ill, health officials trying to uncover the cause found that they had cooked their meals in nonedible oil included in the shipment for nonfood use. The "nonedible" description had failed to get its message across to the villagers.

• A factory was destroyed because a visitor lit his pipe near a container marked "Inflammable Waste." He knew what "flammable" meant and he assumed, logically but inaccurately, that "inflammable" was its opposite.

Each of these incidents stands alone and different from the others, yet there is a clear thread of sameness woven through them all. The sameness linking the incidents together is that each, in its different way, demonstrates the identical point: words can be a two-edged sword.

One edge is a vital tool that cuts a pathway for people toward new understanding and wider knowledge; the other edge is a weapon that turns against them to inflict pain and suffering. In each of these incidents words exposed their weapon edge because they were ambiguous or imprecise, or they were foreign to the reader, or they required a degree of comprehension he did not possess.

So this is the paradox: in the beginning was the word, and in a scriptural sense it has sustained people and has elevated them to spiritual heights ever since, but at the same time words have victimized them.

The trouble began in the remote past when one word led to another—and another—and another at a steadily increasing pace. Soon what had been a verbal trickle became an outpouring—a torrent—a flood. People were being inundated by words that—by their overwhelming number and subtle differences—were making speech into an obstacle course.

The passage of time has merely aggravated the problem. Take a single word—*power*—and see how it jiggles from meaning to meaning like the ball bouncing in a pinball machine. The baseball buff thinks of *power* in terms of a *power* hitter; the carpenter thinks of his *power* tools; the legislator thinks of *power* politics; the mathematician thinks of 64 raised to the tenth *power*; the lawyer thinks of a *power* of attorney; the electrical engineer thinks of a *power* plant; the journalist thinks of the *power* of the press; the laboratory technician thinks of his 10-*power* microscope. That one word, standing alone with nothing to indicate which of its score of meanings is intended, is surely a haphazard route toward clear understanding.

What is true of *power* is true of thousands upon thousands of other words. While the captain in his bridge-deck headquarters *heads* his vessel away from rocky *headland*, the *head* cook is busy in the galley, an off-duty sailor scans the *headlines* in an old newspaper, another sailor goes to the *head* to relieve his bladder, and an argument between two *headstrong* deckhands comes to a *head* when one slugs the other—in the *head*, of course. A *sound* can be a noise or a narrow waterway or an internal organ of a fish; a bank, a horse, or a piece of advice can be *sound*; a doctor uses his stethoscope to *sound* a patient's chest; a football team can be *soundly* trounced, a bored audience can fall *sound* asleep, and a poll can *sound* out public opinion.

Or take two such commonly used words as *hot* and *cold* and see how confusing they can become. You can get *hot* under the collar and break into a *cold* fury all at the same time. Spicy chili con carne placed in a refrigerator is *hot* but it is also *cold*. A trail can grow *cold* on the *hottest* day. The fact is that you can throw a dart at any page in the dictionary and the odds are better than even you will impale a word having the potential for serving man poorly.

It is undeniable that the building blocks of speech— words—too readily become structures sometimes unsafe for human occupancy. But consider how much more hazardous the structure becomes when 5,000 different architects draw the building plans. This is the situation in which the world found itself when words began to arrange themselves into different speech patterns among different peoples and eventually emerged as more than 5,000 separate, distinct languages and dialects. Man, whose words sometimes failed him when he sought to communicate with others who shared his tongue, could now contemplate the likelihood of failure on a five-thousand-fold greater scale. It was an awesome prospect.

One account of the dismemberment of the world into separate language fragments is related in the Biblical story of the Tower of Babel. In Chapter XXI of Genesis, the Lord says: "Behold, the people is one, and they have all one language." But when the people undertook to build a tower reaching to the heavens, an enterprise that was not pleasing to the Lord, He did "confound their language, that they may not understand one another's speech." Confronted by the communications block imposed by this multiplication of languages, the people were forced to abandon the building of their tower and they scattered over the face of the earth.

In their wanderings around the globe, the people managed to take Babel with them wherever they went. No river, no mountain, no national border could stem the invasion of languages. Today Babel is everywhere. English may be the official language of the United States, but for millions of Americans any one of dozens of other tongues is their preferred means of communication. Belgium and Canada each have two official languages: French and English in the case of Canada, French and Flemish in the case of Belgium. Switzerland, small as it is, has four official languages: French, German, Italian, and Romansh. The population of India speaks so many tongues—at least one hundred—that the country has had to turn to English in an effort to find a workable channel of communication within its own borders. A total of nearly 150 different languages are spoken by citizens of the Soviet Union; scarcely more than half of them can understand Russian.

If language can impose a communications barrier within a single country, the barriers become incalculably greater when one seeks to talk across national borders. Even the laborious process of translating back and forth between tongues doesn't always do the trick.

For instance, in the native speech of the tribesmen living in the Sahara oases there are more than 60 different words to designate specific types of palm trees, but there is not a single word for snow. On the other hand, Eskimos have more than 40 words to designate different kinds of snow, but not a single word for a palm tree.

Or consider what happened when the Cleveland Chamber of Commerce tried to create a favorable public image abroad by publicizing the city under its slogan: "Cleveland, the Matchless City." In many places the translation came out: "Cleveland, the City without Matches." Or consider what happened some years ago when the instruction sheet accompanying a shipment of American goods to Russia advised washing in "Ivory Snow." The Russian translation came out: "Wash with soap made from elephant tusks."

In medieval times, travelers and traders in the Western world were so harried by the crippling effect of so many tongues that they invented a new, artificial language—lingua franca—from simplified words and phrases borrowed from French, Spanish, Italian, Arabic, and Greek. The idea behind lingua franca was that enough of a language one was likely to recognize would come through that the meaning of the unfamiliar portions could be guessed.

The conditions that had led traders to invent lingua franca for the Mediterranean basin prevailed wherever man had wandered. On the Pacific island of Leyte—only 120 miles long and averaging about 30 miles in width—natives of the eastern portion could not converse with those on the western side except through an interpreter. In Africa there were more than 700 tongues, in Australia over 200, in Indonesia more than 300.

To overcome the crippling effect of this linguistic bedlam, pidgin languages like the West's lingua franca were created. Usually they were a crude mixture of a European language and two or three of the more widely spoken local tongues, with everything reduced to a bare-bones, stripped-down jargon of the "no tickee, no washee" variety. Along the South China coast it was Chinese-English pidgin. In much of the island chain stretching from Fiji to New Guinea it was Melanesian-English pidgin. The jargon that developed in Zanzibar and Singapore was rooted in Portuguese, in New Caledonia it was based on French, and in Surinam on Dutch.

Pidgin mangles, distorts, and twists language in imaginative ways that amuse and confuse those not attuned to it. Pidgin speakers in Hong Kong say of someone who is crazy, "Have got wata top side." If they want a haircut in New Guinea they say, "Cut 'im grass belong head belong me." If they have a stomachache in Tahiti they complain, "Belly belong me walk about too much." In Australia they call a salesman a "Big fella talk talk watch 'im that one." In Samoa an onion is "Apple belong stink."

Westerners exposed to pidgin for the first time are struck by its childlike logic and simple humor. They usually assume, inaccurately and unjustly, that pidgin speakers are therefore simple, childlike people. After all, pidgin was invented by Westerners. Furthermore, the West has had its full share of pidgin languages in addition to the lingua franca that started it all. Chinook jargon—a mix of English, French, and Indian tongues—thrived in the early years of the American and Canadian northwest as a lingua franca for fur traders and local tribes. Along the South Carolina coast there was, and still is, Gullah—a mixture of African dialects and English. Pennsylvania Dutch, a marriage of German and English that was created when the influx of German immigration to Pennsylvania began in the late seventeenth century, is still widely spoken.

In a very few cases, some pidgin tongues managed eventually to evolve into full-fledged, sophisticated languages. Malay, the national tongue of Indonesia, emerged from a pidgin mixture of several languages spoken by local natives. Swahili, now spoken in a coastal section of East Africa, emerged from a pidginized version of local dialects plus Arabic. Afrikaans, one of the two official languages of the Republic of South Africa (English is the other), is derived from seventeeth century Dutch plus a leavening from languages spoken by local tribesmen.

For almost as long as men have been seeking to improve communication by pidginizing tongues they have also been engaged in a related effort: creation of brand-new, wholly artificial languages complete with their own rules of grammar and vocabularies. By the mid-1600s a half-dozen of these artificial languages had already been constructed. The fact that none of them achieved any measurable degree of popularity or usefulness did not discourage the language inventors. From the seventeenth century until now, something like 700 separate artificial languages have been proposed for international adoption.

Most of these linguistic constructions were too illogical, too complicated, or too freakish to rate serious consideration. One used a combination of both numbers and letters. Another was composed of musical notes. Some were simply unimaginative blends of existing tongues. A few were brilliantly conceived concepts that were impractical for any use beyond a narrow, scholarly circle so that they were really little more than highbrow parlor games.

One artificial language that did receive considerable attention was Volapük, created in Germany a century ago. Its grammar resembled that of German and its vocabulary that of English and Latin. But interest in Volapük waned when its supporters switched their allegiance to a new artificial language—Esperanto—invented by Dr. L. L. Zamenhof in Warsaw in 1887. Esperanto seemed to be promising—its grammar was simple and logical, its pronunciation was uncomplicated, and its vocabulary had mainly Latin, Greek, and German roots so that much of it already had a familiar ring.

Of all the artificial languages Esperanto has come closest to achieving any substantial degree of acceptance. Some 100 newspapers and magazines, all of small circulation, are printed in Esperanto in various parts of the world. By international agreement telegraph stations everywhere are required to accept and transmit telegrams written in Esperanto. Some business houses that actively promote world-wide sales of their products print catalogues in Esperanto. A number of schools around the globe—believed to total about 600 with an enrollment of approximately 20,000—include Esperanto among the subjects they teach. And hundreds of the classics of literature have appeared in Esperanto editions. However, despite these successes fewer than ten million of the global population of more than four billion are able to speak or read Esperanto.

There is an obvious, built-in contradiction surrounding the creation of the hundreds of pidgin and artificial languages that have come into being over the centuries. All were conceived as a means of easing the burden of a world weighed down by an excess of languages, but the very act of their creation increased that already excessive number. It is like trying to smother a fire by piling more wood on it.

While the world was slowly choking on its swollen tongue, people everywhere were becoming more mobile, more interdependent, and more technologically oriented. There was a large measure of absurdity in the situation. On the one hand, the world that was emerging—more compressed in time and space, more industrialized and mechanized—had to depend increasingly upon words to enable it to function. On the other hand, while the world was growing steadily more dependent upon its words, those words were just as steadily growing less dependable.

As though things were not already bad enough, we continued to make matters worse for ourselves by using words in ways that squeezed meaning out of them. Consider this passage from a recent issue of a respected professional journal: "From the consideration of transfer of residual excitation, it can be predicted, then, that humor responses are enhanced not only by excitation which is produced during the time of exposure to humor stimuli but also by residues of excitation caused by a variety of emotional states aroused prior to humor." If the author of that pompous gobbledygook had really wanted his meaning to be understood clearly, he should simply have said, "Jokes get bigger laughs when the listeners are in a lively mood."

It is evident that words, like prices, have become inflated. They get bigger, but they buy less understanding. A brilliant director of the U.S. Geological Survey, Dr. George Otis Smith, put his finger on it back in 1907 when he urged scientists not to become hypnotized by big words, to recognize that more and bigger words simply create more and bigger obstacles to clear communication of ideas.

He warned that words don't make the idea any more than clothes make the man. To drive his point home he waggled a finger of disapproval at his own profession of geology, citing such examples as the use of "space of discontinuity" instead of "crevice," "littoral margin" instead of "shoreline," "argillaceous stratum" instead of "clay," and "arenaceous deposit" instead of "sand."

Today the paradox of a world that can scarcely exist without its words and often can scarcely exist with them poses a dilemma which is creating international alarm. The dilemma becomes more disturbing with each passing day, aggravated by the growing multilingualism of many countries (the United States among them) and by the ever-growing mobility of the world population (more than 200 million people now visit foreign lands each year).

Public safety, health, transportation, education, and social service agencies find that their efforts are being challenged by problems created by words. Political and economic bodies are being hampered by words. Commercial enterprises, manufacturers, and distributors of the world's goods are harassed by words. Those who buy merchandise of every description, who consume products of every character, who use implements, devices, and machines of every type are stumbling over words. Travelers are deflected and side tracked by words.

In short, impediments of speech—both within a single language and among different languages—are preventing understanding between those who offer and those who want to receive important information.

If "normal" people are badgered by "normal" language, the problem is much greater for those with less advantages. These are the handicapped—the mute who cannot speak words, the deaf who cannot hear them, the blind who cannot see them.

In *The Magic Mountain*, the perceptive novelist Thomas Mann observed that "speech is civilization itself." A fundamental truth is that speech is the hallmark of the human condition; people are by their very nature communicators. They are distinguished from all other living creatures by their ability to reason and by their undeniable need to communicate their thoughts and wishes to others.

A second fundamental truth is that the human mind is a marvelously innovative and adaptable instrument: place a barrier before it and it will find a way to surmount the obstacle. Confronted by the basic need to communicate and the frequent limitations of conventional language, people have used their inventive genius to devise communications techniques freeing them from words alone.

There are all sorts of nonverbal languages that convey messages clearly: from the talking drums of Africa to the whistle speech of railroads and tugboats; from the hieroglyphics of the ancients to the pictographs of the Olympics; from the specialized symbol system of music, mathematics, medicine, and other professions to the "public" symbols of traffic signs and religion; from the "touch talk" of the blind to the "hand talk" of the deaf; from smoke signals to the Inca's knots to mariner's flags to beacons to gestures to "body language."

People were not abandoning words nor denying the vastness of the knowledge, truth, and beauty that words can unlock for them. Rather, they were making other keys to use when words stick in the lock.

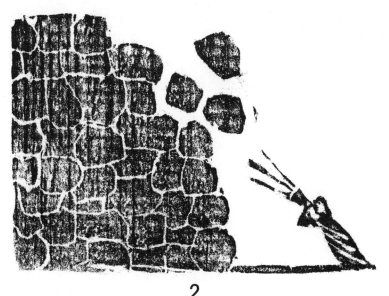

2

Sounding Brass and Tinkling Cymbal

Though I speak with the tongues of men and of angels, and have not charity, I am become as sounding brass, or a tinkling cymbal.

—1 Corinthians, XIII, 1

Among the more curious ways devised to communicate with others is the creation of systems of sounds that resemble conventional speech yet manage to depart from it. Consider, for example, the way the Hottentots and the Bushmen of southwest Africa communicate with one another.

Though they are primitive, pastoral peoples living simple, uncomplicated lives, the Hottentots and Bushmen have nevertheless created a remarkably complex system that is baffling to Western ears. They converse easily by clicking their tongues against their teeth and by emitting throaty purrs. In the subtle variations they introduce into the patterns of their clicks and purrs they are able to satisfy the whole range of their conversational needs.

A related kind of linguistic system was developed by several groups of Pygmies in central Africa and among the Vedda tribesmen of Sri Lanka, formerly known as Ceylon. Though the system developed separately in each place, it is based in both cases on controlled breathing, with communication being accomplished through changes in the pitch, intensity, and rhythm of the breaths. To an eavesdropping outsider a conversation among Pygmies or Veddas is a bewildering mixture of sighs, muted hisses, buzzes, and gentle snores, but it gets its job done effectively. For the Pygmies and the Veddas there is a practical advantage in their unique method of soft, sibilant expression. Both of them are hunting peoples and the low, whisperlike technique enables them to stalk their jungle prey without alarming the animals.

In the Canary Islands communication took a slightly different tack. A group of volcanic islands some 300 miles off the coast of Morocco, the Canaries have had a turbulent history. At various times they were fought over by the Spanish, Dutch, and English, and they were frequently raided by pirates and privateers. The constant upheaval and bloodletting took their toll of the original inhabitants, the Guanches. Not long after the islands became a Spanish dominion in 1496, the weakened, decimated Guanches were absorbed by their conquerors. Though they have long since disappeared, the sounds of the Guanches are still heard on Gomera, one of the Canary islands.

Gomera is a small, mountainous island with deep crevices and rocky precipices. For the Guanches who lived on Gomera the rugged terrain was a formidable barrier to communication. Seeking a way to exchange information past the crags and ravines that separated and silenced them, they created a piercing whistle language that could carry long distances—as much as six or seven miles when atmospheric conditions were right. By varying the pitch and pace of their whistling they were able to conduct complete conversations. The mountains of Gomera have not become any smaller nor the crevices any shallower since the time of the Guanches, so present-day inhabitants continue to converse in the same effective whistle language.

Although nobody can put forth a logical explanation for it, the residents of Kusnoy, a village in Turkey, also employ a whistle language similar to that of Gomera. Whatever it might have been that led them to go in for whistling, they use it routinely for everything from exchanging gossip to discussing crops to arguing village politics. It is even used in Kusnoy to carry on courtships and flirtations. In this respect, at least, the villagers display a marked superiority over those Westerners who have never progressed beyond the solitary message of the "wolf whistle."

One obvious limitation of whistling is that it can deliver its message only as far as the lung power of the sender can propel it. To expand this range, the Ibo tribe of Africa gave their lungs a boost by fashioning clay whistles as amplifiers. When blown, the baked clay whistles emitted a shrill, penetrating call that reached much farther. Skillfully manipulating their instruments, the Ibos blew in controlled patterns that "played" intelligible messages over considerable distances. A number of other tribes achieved similar results using animal bones and horns. Some groups, especially in the islands of the Pacific area, used shells for the same purpose.

From the horns and shells produced by nature, it was only a small step to horns manufactured by man. The Maoris of New Zealand constructed huge horns, many measuring six feet in length, by hollowing out a suitable limb cut from a tree. But the horns created in Tibet dwarfed those of the Maoris. Frequently as long as 12 feet, they were fashioned of brass and were used for communication between widely separated settlements in that remote, mountainous country.

The carrying power and flexibility with which sounds could be adjusted into easily recognizable patterns made wind instruments attractive devices. Long before the dawn of Christianity, many peoples—the Greeks, Chinese and Romans among them—had adopted a variety of horns and trumpets as a means of signalling. The Bible itself records the frequent use of trumpets for that purpose. The Biblical account of Joshua's siege of Jericho recounts that the blare of trumpets brought down the walls of the city.

As widespread as was the use of horns and trumpets, drums were more commonly used to send messages to distant ears. From the Congo region deep in Africa to the islands dotting the Pacific Ocean to the Amazon basin deep in South America, drums did for a large part of the world what Bell Telephone and Western Union set out to do in a much later era. There were drums of every conceivable description: big, little and in-between sizes; drums made from logs, gourds, and pottery; drums covered with animal skins and drums covered with animal intestines; drums that were rubbed, pounded by hand, beaten with sticks; drums for ceremonial occasions and for routine purposes.

There was scarcely a part of Africa—especially in the vast bulk of the continent south of the Sahara—that did not echo with the throb and boom of the talking drums. To refer to them as talking drums is not to indulge in a flight of fancy: they were so versatile and the operators so skilled that they could virtually talk.

Many of the Congo tribes fashioned their drums from sections of tree trunks as long as eight feet and as thick as four. To give this huge block of wood its voice, craftsmen cut a narrow, lengthwise slit in one of its sides and reached through it to laboriously hollow out the interior. Working carefully and patiently, they transformed the thick log into a great, resonating sound chamber that was enclosed everywhere except for the slit. To play the drum, the operator struck it across the slit with either one or two sticks. The pulsating sounds he created thundered their message through the jungle for as many as 12 miles.

Some tribes opened one end of their log drums and stretched an animal skin—often a dried elephant's ear— over the opening. By altering the tension of the vines that bound the skin over the opening, the operator could alter the pitch of the sound he beat out of it.

A few African tribes—the Ashanti and the Bagandi among them—almost always used their drums in pairs, one designed to emit low-pitched sounds, the other giving out high-pitched ones. The operator could vary the pitch further according to how close to its center or edge he struck the drumhead and according to the strength of his blows. The variety of the pitches, together with the pace and rhythm of his blows, gave the drummer the flexibility he needed to transmit complex, detailed information. Thus—with hollowed logs, animal skins, and skillful hands, and with an understanding between drummer and listener of what the various patterns of sounds meant— tribes could exchange information on a wide range of matters. Tribes that were dispersed over a large area established repeating stations to reproduce their messages and pass them along, making it the jungle's equivalent of the typist pounding out carbon copies. Some of these talking drums continue to throb out their messages today in some parts of Africa even though newer forms of communicating exist.

Slit drums similar to those of Africa were also common in the Fiji Islands, the Solomons, New Guinea, New Caledonia, and other Pacific Ocean islands. These South Sea drums ranged in size from three footers to giants fifteen and sixteen feet long. On several of the islands the drum talk was so highly organized that each family had its own call signal so the drums could be used to converse with a specific individual, much like today's CBs are used. Of course, just as in the case of CB conversations, everybody else within range could listen in even though the message was not intended for them.

The Aztecs of Central America and a number of Indian tribes along the Amazon regularly used talking drums. These were usually slit drums similar to those of Africa and the Pacific islands, but considerably smaller—seldom more than four or five feet long.

These primitive techniques are still apparent today in our so-called sophisticated society.

Take tongue-clicking, for instance. A common way of signifying "no" in the Middle East is to make a clucking sound with tongue against teeth. And in Italy when a man clucks at a passing girl he is delivering the same message that street-corner Romeos transmit by other means in other places. We think nothing of clucking out a "tsk-tsk" to indicate "Isn't that a shame?" and a "tut-tut" to indicate "Don't worry about it."

Even the breathing communication of the Pygmy has its modern counterpart in the "uh-huh" that we use for a positive response and in the "uh-uh" that we use for a negative response. Furthermore, in the way we adjust our breath control, rhythm, and emphasis we can cause that "uh-huh" to express doubt, reluctant agreement, distrust, or hesitation instead of merely a straightforward "yes." In a similar manner we can enlarge the vocabulary of our "uh-uh" to make it mean more than just a simple "no." For variety, we often emit a drawn-out humming "mmmm" that doesn't commit us one way or the other while it gains time for us to consider what to decide. And we hiss to express our displeasure or give a "Bronx cheer" to voice scorn. You might say there is a lot of Pygmy in all of us.

As for whistling, any railroad man would feel an instant kinship with the residents of Gomera and Kusnoy because railroaders have long shared a whistle language of their own. As a regular part of their working routine they blast out a variety of operational information in the piercing blare of their engine whistles. Three short blasts and one long tell the flagman to go to the head of the train; one long and three shorts send him to the rear; two longs signify that the train is about to move forward; three shorts say it is about to move backward. Railroaders, unlike the people in Kusnoy, may not be able to conduct a courtship with their whistling but they do keep their trains functioning with it.

In fact whistling is a common means of communication when you get right down to it. Organized sports would quickly become disorganized without the whistling communication from the officials to the players. Police whistles tell the motorist what to do and when to do it. Factories change shifts in response to whistles. The working language of vessels plying the world's waterways is whistle talk. Sirens—which are only whistles that know how to flex their muscles—clear the road for emergency vehicles, signal civil defense tests, announce mine disasters, and report break-ins by burglars.

Only slightly removed from whistles and sirens are the assorted bells, horns, and buzzers that deliver their multitude of varied instructions and information. They get us up in the morning, tell the cook to turn the stove off, send the student from one classroom to another, warn the mariner of hazards at sea, tell the typist she is getting close to the margin, and alert firemen to the outbreak of a fire and then describe to them the degree of its severity. Surely those are a demonstration of impressive fluency.

Even the wooden horn of the New Zealand Maoris plays a role in modern life. In the Swiss Alps, where the steep terrain makes it a very fatiguing, time-consuming chore to round up grazing cattle on remote slopes, farmers blow *alpenhorn* to call their cows back to the barn. The summons of these wooden horns, many as long as twelve feet, easily penetrates the thin, mountain air to the most distant cattle and tells them it is time to come home. And the trumpeters at Jericho would appreciate the role of buglers in modern armies around the world. More than forty different messages are delivered to soldiers via bugle calls, although the two that please them most probably are pay call and mess call.

Putting together all the whistles, bells, horns, trumpets, drums, you have one of the most subtle forms of communication modern society employs: music. It delivers a powerful message to all peoples everywhere. The sounds of a national anthem, a hymn, a lullaby stir the emotions. A spirited march or a school "fight" song gets the adrenaline flowing. A funeral dirge conveys its sense of sorrow. Music can calm or arouse. It can inspire, amuse, motivate, inflame, refresh. As Longfellow wrote, "Music is the universal language of mankind."

3

What You See Is What You Get

There was speech in their dumbness, language in their very gesture.

—William Shakespeare

Early in history, man communicated by the most natural and spontaneous of all methods—gestures. Nothing is more instinctive than to clutch your stomach and grimace to indicate a bellyache; to open your eyes wide in terror to reveal fear; or to raise your hand threateningly to signal anger. Most linguists agree that communication by gestures preceded speech—probably for hundreds of thousands of years before intelligible speech became common.

The science of gestural communication is called pasimology. Authorities in this field believe that facial expressions, body positions, and finger, hand, and arm movements—either alone or in various combinations—can create a remarkable 700,000 separate gestures. When that awesome total is compared with the normal vocabulary of the average individual—a mere few thousand words—it seems that gestures could be used to convey anything the human mind conceives.

Even after oral speech began, gestures continued in extensive use. Often they were a supplement to the spoken word, but sometimes they remained the sole means of communication. The language of the Arunta Bushmen of central Australia, for instance, consisted entirely of a highly developed system of hand signs. In parts of Asia and Africa natives regularly used gestures to augment their speech, especially when dealing with clans whose spoken languages were different from theirs. Gestural communication played a lively role in Europe, particularly in southern Europe where it is still very much in evidence. Scores of Indian tribes through North and South America conversed with one another readily despite their bewildering multiplicity of tongues because they had created a comprehensive system of hand signs. Even today Indians living in and around the town of Otavalo in Ecuador are known as the "quiet" Indians because they do all their marketing exclusively in signs.

Students of pasimology recall how gestures enabled King Ferdinand of Naples to save both his head and crown. One day in 1821 Ferdinand's palace was surrounded by an angry throng of citizens who sought to end his reign. In trying to pacify them Ferdinand went out to address them from a palace balcony, but his words were lost in the uproar. So Ferdinand switched from words to gestures and conveyed clearly to the mob a long message that combined conciliation, threats, and promises. The people understood him and went home.

Gestures are very much a part of today's world. People in dozens of occupations use them. Orchestra conductors speak to their musicians through their hands. At construction sites the operators of heavy equipment jockey their mechanical monsters in response to hand signals. Gestures are a language of the auction house. Commodities speculators on the floor of the Chicago Board of Trade use hand movements to buy and sell millions of dollars' worth of everything from soy beans to gold to plywood. Using hand signals alone, croupiers in the gambling casinos in Monte Carlo inform each other about deadbeats, request replenishment of their table banks, ask the floor manager for help, and pass along other information. Armies have an extensive system of gestures they can use to conduct scouting missions, issue firing commands, assemble troops, operate tanks, and perform other military functions. Umpires and referees in football, baseball, and a dozen other major sports rely on hand signals for communication among themselves and with players and spectators. Performers of the traditional dances of Japan, China, Korea, Hawaii, and Indonesia use gestural language to explain to their audiences the story of each dance.

Occasionally gestures can even become news stories that make headlines. When former Vice President Nelson A. Rockefeller was being heckled by demonstrators he responded by jabbing the middle finger of one of his hands up into the air, a gesture that is recognized internationally as both insulting and vulgar. An Associated Press photographer snapped a picture of the gesturing vice president which appeared in newspapers and magazines throughout the country.

Some months later a woman in Austin, Texas, was arrested on a charge of disorderly conduct when she "gave the finger" to some policemen. The arrested woman's attorney insisted that gestures are a legitimate form of communication protected by the freedom of speech guarantee of the First Amendment of the Constitution. Apparently there was merit in the defense, for the court acquitted the defendant.

"Giving the finger" supposedly originated with Diogenes, the Greek philosopher, more than 2,000 years ago. Diogenes is said to have been attending a speech being delivered by Demosthenes in Athens and to have become so upset over statements by the famous orator that he thrust his middle finger into the air as a sign of his displeasure and contempt.

Gestures have been the subject of legislative deliberation. For a long time Germans displayed anger toward someone by flashing him the "cuckoo" sign—tapping a finger against one's forehead. Motorists, especially, used the rude gesture to insult one another and taunt pedestrians. The widespread custom caused so much anger that officials realized road safety was in peril. Finally a law was passed banning the gesture in public.

There is more to gestural communication than mere "hand talk." Charlie Chaplin, Sigmund Freud, and Cicero all knew that. It is hard to imagine a more diverse trio— the first a giant of early Hollywood movies, the second the founder of psychoanalysis in nineteenth century Vienna, and the third the greatest orator of the Roman Empire of 2,000 years ago. Yet all understood that the entire body can be an articulate vehicle for expression.

Cicero, teaching would-be Roman orators the fine points of effective communication, urged them to use "the language of the body which is understood even by savages and barbarians."

Freud was convinced people speak more eloquently with their bodies than with words. Though a man might clamp his lips shut, Freud insisted, his innermost secret "oozes out of him at every pore."

Charlie Chaplin and fellow pioneers of the silent screen—with their mugging, posturing, pantomiming, scowling, leering—had no difficulty in projecting their thoughts and emotions to audiences around the world.

Even without movement of any kind the body is capable of conveying information. An erect carriage, shoulders squared, chest out, head up, speaks of confidence and pride; slumped, head down, shoulders sagged, it transmits an opposite message. Kneeling, the body delivers the universal sign of submission. In motion the body becomes remarkably fluent. A firm stride marks the leader; a shuffle reveals the follower. Cockiness is communicated by walking with a bouncy step, upper body leaning ahead, arms swinging in an exaggerated arc, or by sitting in a sprawl and thrusting the feet forward. The sexual message comes across clearly in a pelvic-thrusting, hip-swiveling walk. Merely by they way they walked, a Jack Benny could deliver a message of humor, a Nazi storm trooper a message of violence and malice, a Marilyn Monroe a message of passion.

Each part of the body speaks. Shrugging the shoulders speaks of indifference. Foot tapping communicates impatience. Knuckle cracking conveys nervousness. Flexing the muscles delivers a "macho" message. Stroking the chin slowly indicates thought. In the way they move the parts of their bodies pantomimists like the masterful Marcel Marceau can relate long, involved sequences of events so that they are clearly understood even though not a word has been spoken.

The face is especially eloquent. It can reveal one's thoughts, emotions, and attitudes with great accuracy. Eyes "light up" to reveal pleasure, open wide to indicate surprise, roll to expose terror, narrow and shift to suggest evasiveness, wander slowly to reveal a lack of interest, lower demurely to signal shyness, stare boldly to expose aggression. The eyes can flirt, pity, forgive, challenge, hate, beg, love.

The brow can arch up in surprise. The lid can blink in nervousness or wink in conspiracy. A forehead can wrinkle in puzzlement and a chin can be pushed out pugnaciously. The lips can part to reveal stress or fear or clamp together to signal disapproval. The bottom lip can be extended as a sign of determination. Lips can turn down in a frown, tremble in fear, curl in scorn, and purse in wonder.

Automatically we nod our head for "yes," shake it from side to side for "no," and touch thumb to forefinger to form a circle indicating "okay." Yet the public gestures we use so freely don't always mean the same things everywhere.

Consider how "yes" and "no" can trap the unwary. Among Arabs and Bulgarians "yes" is signaled by the sideways shake of the head that means "no" in the United States and most Western countries. In southern Italy, however, "no" is usually an upward sweep of the head while at the same time the lower lip is pushed out, and in Turkey and many parts of the Middle East "no" is an upward sweep of the head coupled with a clucking of the tongue. Among the Punjabis of India, a sharp upward sweep of the head means "yes," but among Sri Lankans "yes" is signified by tilting the head downward toward the left shoulder. The upshot of all of this is that one man's "yes" can very well be the next man's "no," and vice versa.

Now consider the American custom of touching thumb to forefinger to mean "okay." In Brazil that is a vulgar gesture far from okay in polite society. Brazilians signal "okay" by extending a thumb upward. But the thumbing motion that gets hitchhikers a ride in most places gets them only an angry look in Scotland and Australia where it is an insulting sign.

There is a curious history surrounding the "thumbs

down" gesture that is widely acknowledged to be a mark of disapproval. It had its origin in ancient Rome in the violent contests that pitted gladiator against gladiator in brutal combat. Contest officials who felt that a defeated gladiator had not fought fiercely enough expressed their disapproval by giving the thumb gesture as a signal that the loser was to be put to death. But in those days the thumb was pointed up instead of down. Why, when, or by whom the position was reversed is anybody's guess.

Even comings and goings can develop a split personality. If the French or Italians raise a hand toward you, palm outward, and flutter their fingers up and down they are signaling "come here," but in the United States that is the good-bye gesture. However, when Americans raise a hand, palm facing inward, and flutter their fingers up and down to signal "come here" they are unwittingly using the French and Italian gesture for "goodbye."

Another oddity is presented by the clenched fist raised up and shaken at somebody. Virtually everywhere it is instantly recognized as an indication of deep anger. However, among tribesmen in northern Nigeria it is employed as a friendly greeting. 2007349

Early in the eleventh century Scandinavians began composing sagas—oral narratives—recounting the exploits of actual or mythical figures. One of the sagas demonstrates that even in medieval Scandinavia gestures could produce unexpected results. According to the saga, a debate took place between a one-eyed Viking and a holy man, each communicating entirely by gestures. At one point in the silent debate the holy man raised a single finger. The Viking raised two in response. The holy man countered with three fingers. Whereupon the Viking raised a fist and the debating broke off.

A spectator asked the holy man to explain what the gestures had meant. "I raised one finger," he responded, "to indicate that God is one. My opponent disputed me by displaying two fingers to show that besides God, the Father, there is also God, the Son. To let him know that his theology is incomplete I raised three fingers because there is a Godly Trinity: Father, Son, and Holy Spirit. But this man is a wily debater. When he made a fist to show that the Trinity is one in God I could not argue any further."

When the Viking was asked for his version of the debate he said, "It had nothing at all to do with God. When my opponent raised one finger he was mocking me because I have only one eye. I countered with two fingers to indicate that my one eye is the equal of his two. He continued to snicker at me by raising three fingers to show that between both of us we have only three eyes, so I raised a fist to let him know what he could expect if he persisted in mocking me."

Though this saga preserves what is only a legend, it does make the valid point that gestures can deliver a garbled message if sender and receiver do not use the same gestures in the same way. There is a modern counterpart to the Scandinavian tale of misunderstood fingers. Almost everywhere "four" could be indicated by an upraised hand with thumb tucked in and the four fingers extended. But in Japan that means "one" because the only digits the Japanese count are those that are folded in across the palm. To indicate "four" in Japan requires extending the thumb outward and tucking the fingers in over the palm.

Pasimology is a thriving, expanding field that is gaining new international importance. It may seem unlikely—particularly in this age of instant communication via orbiting satellite—that learned scientific bodies in such widely separated places as Denmark, Israel, Pakistan, and the United States would perceive the old hand signs of the American Indian as a technique worthy of modern application. But they do. After you discover Madge Skelly you understand why.

An Iroquois Indian born in Pittsburgh, Madge Skelly has been a stage, radio, and television actress, and an instructor in public speaking at the University of Arizona. Now, in her mid-seventies, Dr. Skelly is a double professor at St. Louis University: professor of speech disorders *and* professor of community medicine. Widely sought as a lecturer to learned bodies around the world, she has drawn on her unique background—Indian, actress, speech pathologist—to help people who have lost the power of speech to communicate easily. To help such people she has created Amerind, a version of Indian hand signs.

Dr. Skelly is quick to point out that Amerind is not a sign system for the deaf, but a signal system for the hearing who have become speechless. The possibility of resurrecting the hand talk of her ancestors came to her more than a dozen years ago when she was working with a patient who had lost the lower part of his face to cancer and could communicate only by writing time-consuming notes. Dr. Skelly vaguely remembered some of the hand signs her grandfather had taught her in childhood. She recalled how graphic and understandable they had seemed and she knew they had been the means whereby Indians of different tribes had readily bridged the language differences separating them. Why couldn't those graphic signs be used to enable people like her patient to make their basic needs and wishes known without resorting to the laborious process of writing? Furthermore, it could work anywhere regardless of the local tongue.

Madge Skelly sought out the aging chiefs of the Iroquois, the Navaho, the Apache, and the Chippewa who still remembered the old ways and from them she learned the hand signals they knew. To these she added other signs she was able to glean from historic documents in museums and other centers of learning. Analyzing her collection, she discarded those that no longer applied in a modern society and developed new ones where gaps appeared. So far her Amerind contains some 200 signs that she has taught to scores of speech pathologists who, in turn, have taught them to more than 500 speechless patients. It has opened up a new, significant channel of communication for them. This accomplishment has stimulated the surge of invitations to Dr. Skelly to introduce Amerind across the United States and in many countries abroad.

Amerind signs are so logical and easily understood that with minimum effort the speechless user can make his meaning clear to almost anyone.

For instance, if someone points a finger at himself, then raises his hands, palms together, and rests his head against them, you quickly understand he is tired and wants to sleep.

If he follows this with the classic sign for "shelter"—hands raised with only the fingertips touching so that they form a tentlike shape—and looks at you with a questioning expression, you understand he is asking where he can find a place to sleep.

If he goes through this sequence but modifies it by pointing at you instead of himself you realize he is asking where you sleep, or to put it another way, where you live.

So Amerind is both simple and flexible. It provides the speechless with an easy means of expressing basic concepts. But it is not, nor is it intended to be, a technique for the free-flowing delivery of ideas and abstractions.

For the deaf, communication is considerably more complicated than for the speechless who are able to hear. In the United States alone about 14 million persons suffer severely impaired hearing. Of these, more than two million are totally deaf, a quarter of them "prelingually deaf," that is, their inability to hear began at birth or during infancy before they started learning to speak.

Thus, the prelingually deaf have never absorbed the sounds of words or the ways letters and combinations of letters are pronounced. Speaking is an imitative process, a matter of duplicating the speech one listens to—which is why a Southerner sounds like a Southerner and a Yankee like a Yankee. However, those who have never listened to speech cannot know what it is they are supposed to mimic. They cannot know the things learned so effortlessly in childhood by every hearing person: the ways to use tongue, lips, and vocal chords to produce recognizable, understandable words. So the tragedy of the prelingually deaf is compounded into an inability either to absorb or to produce normal speech.

The world of the silent is drab, empty, frustrating, and dangerous in ways that hearing persons cannot appreciate. A shouted warning, a fire alarm, the squealing of automobile brakes, the buzzing around a nest of angry wasps, a doorbell—all are unheard and so unheeded. A telephone is no longer a link to the doctor and the police, to shops and repairmen, to family and friends. Movies and television are arid, lifeless experiences. The radio has no voice.

A priest in eighteenth century France, Abbé Charles Michel de l'Eppe, disturbed because deaf children in his parish were unable to receive religious instruction, cast about for a way to break through their wall of silence to bring them the teachings of the Church. Watching the children and pondering the problem, he observed that they were able to communicate among themselves by making gestures and hand signals. He also realized that Trappist monks—to avoid breaking their vow of silence

—used signs for necessary communication among themselves.

So the priest—just as Dr. Skelly was to do with Indian signs two centuries later—gathered together the signals of the children and the monks and built on them to create a formal system of communication by hand. An enlarged form of this hand language is used today by most of the deaf in the United States to converse with one another and with hearing persons who have learned the system. Each gesture in sign language stands for a specific word or for an entire short sentence. This is supplemented by a manual alphabet in which each letter is indicated by arranging the fingers in a particular position. Words for which there are no signs are spelled out in the alphabetical finger positions.

Any who doubt the capacity of this system to function as a full-fledged language should visit the attractive campus of Gallaudet College in Washington, D.C. Founded in 1864 by an act of Congress, Gallaudet is a fully accredited senior college offering a regular liberal arts curriculum. Its 1,000 students come from all parts of the United States and more than 20 foreign nations. What distinguishes Gallaudet from every other liberal arts college in the world is that every one of its students and more than 25 percent of its faculty are deaf.

All subjects at Gallaudet—sciences, humanities, arts— are taught in signs. Furthermore, the students engage in a full range of extracurricular activities—sports, clubs, hobbies—in which signing replaces speaking. To see the students gyrating and capering out on the dance floor like collegians on any campus surprises first-time visitors. Although the Gallaudet dancers can't hear the music, they feel the vibrations of the beat and keep time to it flawlessly.

The college drama club is especially popular, staging

signed comedies as well as serious plays. To witness truly superb signed productions one should visit the National Theater of the Deaf (NTD), a professional acting company established in Connecticut in 1967. It has played to enthusiastic audiences in all fifty states and in Europe, Asia, Australia, and the Middle East. NTD emphasizes that it is a theater *of* the deaf, not simply *for* the deaf, and usually fully 85 percent of its audiences are hearing. To accommodate the hearing who have no knowledge of signs, two or three hearing actors are integrated into the on-stage action to speak the lines being signed by the deaf actors. But the signs themselves match the stage action so well and are delivered with such theatrical clarity and emphasis that they actually enhance the meaning of the spoken lines for the hearing audience.

In its first decade of professional life the NTD has given more than 2,000 performances and been hailed for adding a new dimension to the stage by bringing to it the beauty and expressiveness of "visual language." NTD has now spawned the Little Theater of the Deaf which consists of three small, traveling troupes—each composed of four deaf actors and one hearing speaker—so that deaf theater can play to a greatly expanded audience.

Perhaps an even more forceful demonstration of the flexibility and versatility of sign language as a means of communication is its role in worship. Scores of churches and synagogues conduct signed services for deaf congregations. Children are baptized, christened, confirmed, and bar mitzvahed in signs. Marriage vows are exchanged, rituals performed, sermons delivered, blessings bestowed, prayers offered in signs. But sign language does more than simply serve to convey the emotions, the concepts, and the abstractions of religion. It adds a new sensitivity to worship, heightening the beauty and spirituality of the traditional rites. There is graceful poetry in the sign for the Lord: a fluid sweep of the hand toward heaven. A shimmering of the fingers denotes fire. The coming of the Lord is a gently flowing gesture that suggests an embrace.

The Interdenominational Church Ushers Association is now introducing a new role for signing in religion: silent communication among ushers to enable them to perform their duties during church services without disturbing either the congregation or the pastor. Using inconspicuous gestures originated by the Association, ushers exchange information among themselves, asking and answering questions, and passing along instructions wordlessly. The gestural language of ushering has proven so useful that the Association has established a school in Washington to teach it and has already graduated more than 2,000 student ushers.

Sign language capable of delicate, sensitive communication on a spiritual plane can also afford blunt communication in practical politics. This was evident in the 1976 presidential campaign when Jimmy Carter habitually arranged for an interpreter to appear on the platform with him to translate his important speeches into sign as he delivered them. Interestingly, it was during the Ford-Carter television debates in Philadelphia that more than 75 million hearing Americans gained an inkling of the frustrations of deafness when the television sound system failed for twenty-six minutes. Watching their animated but silent screens, the audience also learned something else: trying to read lips is an exercise in futility. The deaf have long known that even after intensive training a skilled lip reader is lucky if he can recognize even one-third of the words spoken.

A number of pasimologists urge the worldwide adoption of hand signs as an international language for everyone—the hearing and the deaf, the speechless and the speaking—to facilitate communication among all peoples regardless of native tongue or of physical limitation. They emphasize the ease with which the deaf employ signs as an effective substitute for the spoken language and point out American Indian sign language as an example of easy, silent communication among the hearing. Pasimologists also cite the Boy Scouts' adoption of Indian signs as their official international language. Boy Scouts from scores of different countries, meeting at international jamborees, conduct business sessions as well as "bull" sessions in sign without much difficulty.

The proposal of gestural language for general, world-wide use is not new. Charles Darwin, the eminent British naturalist, made a serious evaluation of the proposal more than a century ago. Darwin agreed that signs have a tremendous capacity for conveying information of every character, on all levels and among people of all backgrounds. However, he concluded, two limitations tend to diminish the usefulness of the system: it can be "spoken" only when the hands are free, and it can be "heard" only when there is sufficient light and an unobstructed view of the hands.

4

Of Rosetta Stones and McDonald's Arches

From shadows and symbols into the truth.
— John Henry, Cardinal Newman.

During a visit to Moscow a few years ago Dr. Jack Adams-Ray, a noted Swedish surgeon, stumbled while crossing Red Square. As he sprawled heavily on the pavement, a searing pain in his left leg snatched his breath away. Unable to rise, he was comforted by passers-by who summoned an ambulance.

At the hospital Dr. Adams-Ray's medical training enabled him to appreciate the high quality of the emergency procedures that were initiated for the severe kneecap injury he had sustained; he complimented the Soviet doctor in English, the only language they shared in common. But after he had been wheeled from the treatment room to his hospital bed, the Swedish surgeon was helplessly inarticulate amid the Russian-speaking ward staff. Because he could not speak Russian he could not ask that the position of his leg be adjusted, or request a bedpan, or explain that the knife thrusts of pain—temporarily dulled by medication—were again stabbing him.

The irony of his unhappy situation was not lost on Dr. Adams-Ray. Fluent in eight languages other than Russian, an emeritus professor of surgery in Sweden's prestigious Karolinska Institute, he was nevertheless unable to communicate on his own behalf despite his language and medical skills. For the first time in his life he realized that a language "fracture" could, like a bone fracture, inflict real suffering on its victim.

In the following days he thought often of the need to find a way to prevent conventional speech from becoming a complicating factor in the practice of medicine. A possible solution occurred to him when he recalled an evening he had spent watching a spirited performance by the Bolshoi Ballet. The intricacies of the Bolshoi dances could be communicated clearly to ballet performers everywhere via a language-free system of symbols. In the method devised by ballet to escape the limitations of conventional language might lie the solution he was seeking for medicine.

Returning to Sweden, Dr. Adams-Ray compiled a long list of all of the more common situations likely to arise in a doctor-patient relationship. Then he created simple, graphic, cartoonlike representations to depict those situations. He tested his cartoons on professional colleagues and patients, until satisfied they could fully comprehend the message of each drawing without need of verbal explanations. With his imaginative cartoon booklet he had succeeded in bridging the word gap separating medical staffs and patients who share no common tongue.

Even subtle meanings are conveyed by the Adams-Ray booklet. Do you have a headache? Point to the cartoon of the grimacing character whose head is encircled by "pain stars" as a hammer strikes it. *Terrible* headache? Point to the character who emits more, bigger stars as his head is struck by a bigger, heavier hammer. Today the booklet is in use as a valuable medical tool in hundreds of hospitals and clinics around the world where staffs and patients are likely to speak different tongues.

In turning to symbols to solve a medical problem Dr. Adams-Ray was utilizing a technique that stretched back into antiquity. From earliest times people have often turned to pictographs and glyphs to get a message across. The ancient Chinese, who had a proverb to suit almost every occasion, originated the still-popular expression: "One picture is worth ten thousand words."

A pictograph is a representational symbol clearly suggesting the thing it stands for—like a bounding deer for a deer crossing, or like Dr. Adams-Ray's character with his headache. A glyph, also called a hieroglyphic, is either abstract or arbitrary. If it is abstract, the glyph vaguely suggests the thing it stands for—like wavy, horizontal, blue lines for water, and like a jagged line for lightning. If it is arbitrary, the glyph does not in any way resemble the thing it stands for—like a dollar sign, or the Red Cross symbol—but its meaning is nevertheless clear once it is learned and memorized.

Among the most enthusiastic of the early practitioners of communication via symbols were the ancient Egyptians. Numerous examples of their symbol system survived them, but understanding of how the system functioned disappeared with them. For centuries all efforts to decipher the written record they had left behind failed because their symbols were a baffling mixture of pictographs, abstract glyphs, and arbitrary glyphs. Missing was any hint of how one symbol related to another, and without that knowledge, understanding of the system was impossible. Then help arrived from an unexpected source: Napoleon Bonaparte.

Although Napoleon is remembered for his military genius, he had intellectual curiosity about many things. When he led an invading army into Egypt in 1798 he took with him a team of 100 of France's leading scholars. The major task Bonaparte assigned to this group was to fan out over the conquered territory to compile complete, precise descriptions of Egypt's ancient monuments, concentrating particularly on the perplexing hieroglyphics carved on them. The findings of the team of scholars filled nineteen massive volumes and brought together a vast wealth of data, but failed to uncover the secret of decoding the hieroglyph system.

Then one of the French engineer detachments constructing a fortified position on the Nile near the town of Rosetta unearthed a section of black stone covered with curious inscriptions. The detachment commander had the good sense to judge that his find, which came to be called the Rosetta Stone, should receive expert attention.

Study of the Rosetta Stone revealed that it bore three distinctly different kinds of inscriptions: one in hieroglyphics, one in a simplified form of the hieroglyphics, and the third in old Greek. Here was a fresh enigma. Why three different kinds of inscriptions? Jean F. Champollion, a language scholar, puzzled over the problem until an answer came to him. Each inscription recorded the same text, each in its own way. With mounting excitement Champollion worked out a careful translation of the old Greek, which he was able to understand. Then, drawing upon his scholarly intuition and training and using the Greek translation as a guide, he set out to break down the other inscriptions symbol by symbol and ferret out their meanings. Eventually he succeeded in reconstructing the way the system functioned. The riddle of Egyptian hieroglyphics had finally been solved.

American archeologists regard the Rosetta Stone with understandable envy. For a long time they have been searching fruitlessly for a way to solve the baffling mystery of the California petroglyphs. The petroglyphs— symbolized drawings on rocks ("petro" is Greek for "rock")—exist in several places in the southern California desert region. For many years scientists have struggled unsuccessfully to interpret their meanings. All they have been able to determine so far is that they were drawn by an ancient Indian civilization about 12,000 years ago and that most seem to tell stories about that long-vanished culture. The investigators are tantalized by the petroglyphic messages from a people who lived in California one hundred centuries before the Christian era began. Who were those ancient Americans? What do their rock drawings say? The answers elude the experts. But persistence, skill, and a large measure of luck may yet reveal them.

Recently a brilliant Soviet scholar was able to crack the hieroglyphic system of the Mayas who once occupied Central America. Spanish *conquistadores* overran the Mayas in the sixteenth century, persecuting and decimating them and destroying their writings. All knowledge of how to read the Mayan symbols died in the flames and pillage that consumed the Mayans and their writings. But two centuries later three Mayan manuscripts that had somehow escaped the *conquistador* bonfires surfaced in Europe. The three priceless manuscripts ended up carefully preserved in museums—one in Madrid, one in Paris, and the third in Dresden—where they languished decade after decade.

In the 1940s a linguistics expert in Leningrad, Dr. Yuri Knorozov, intrigued by the mystery of the Mayan relics, secured copies of them. With disciplined patience and academic insights Dr. Knorozov labored over the manuscripts in a cubbyhole office in a Soviet museum. Slowly, fragment by fragment, he chipped away the enigma of the Mayan hieroglyphics. Now, after a quarter of a century of dedicated effort, he has succeeded in decoding the Mayan system, triumphing over the flames to which the *conquistadores* had consigned it.

A prime reason that decoding both the Mayan and the Egyptian systems had been such long, arduous tasks is that they were complete written languages—total systems for comprehensive, general-purpose communication on any subject. Each had its own principles of grammar and its own rules governing the ways in which its thousands of symbols were to be employed. Thus, to read the glyphs the Egyptians and Mayas left behind demanded not only a knowledge of the symbol meanings themselves but also a detailed knowledge of how they related to one another.

But over the long span of his years on earth, man has also developed many less complicated symbol systems designed for specialized purposes. Because they were intended for specific, limited uses they succeeded in accomplishing their aims with far fewer symbols and rules. Dr. Adams-Ray's booklet—and the ballet glyphs that inspired it—are examples of simplified, limited-purpose forms. There are literally scores of others in widespread daily use to satisfy the special needs of special groups regardless of their native tongues—the proofreader's marks of printers and editors, the weather symbols of meterologists, the zodiac glyphs of astrologers, the blueprints of plumbers. All of these different groups, besides scientists, mechanics, tradesmen, engineers, mariners, aviators, and a host of others, depend on special-purpose symbol systems peculiar to their own professions.

A few special symbol systems cut across occupational

lines to serve a much broader group. Of these the most universal of course is the language of numbers. Every culture throughout recorded history has experienced an inescapable need for a way to indicate quantities exactly. The Egyptians met that need by creating hieroglyphics for the numerals one through ten and for the powers of ten (ten to the second power, or ten times ten; ten to the third power, or ten times ten times ten, and so on).

To indicate "two thousand five hundred fifty-five," for example, the citizen of old Egypt commenced with the glyph for ten to the third power, which looked like this ⟊ . Because this represented only one thousand (ten times ten times ten), he repeated the symbol a second time to increase the value to two thousand. Next, to represent five hundred, the glyph for one hundred (ten to the second power) was reproduced five times—

99999   —and then the glyph for ten was inscribed five times to indicate fifty: ∩∩∩∩∩ Finally, the mark for five was added to the row of symbols: ⦀ . So to indicate two thousand five hundred fifty-five the Egyptian of antiquity wrote:

⟊⟊ 99999 ∩∩∩∩∩ ⦀

Though it served the purpose, it was a clumsy arrangement requiring the awkward repetition of many identical glyphs. The number method later devised by the Romans reduced the need for so much repetition. The Romans used letters for the powers of ten (X for ten, C for one hundred, M for one thousand) and for numbers based on five (V for five, L for fifty, and D for five hundred). So the Roman could write two thousand five hundred fifty-five as: MMDLV.

Other early cultures, such as the Babylonian, the Mayan, and the Greek had their own distinctive symbol systems to convey information relating to quantity, but all had various shortcomings. The Greeks, for instance, had to memorize more than two dozen separate symbols merely to express quantities smaller than one thousand.

One of the early systems was that devised by the Hindus of India over 2,000 years ago. Its symbols were crudely shaped, but gradually, with usage, they became refined, streamlined, easy to write. However, what made it unique among all numbering systems was a revolutionary concept that later Hindu scholars introduced into it: the idea of nothingness, of a void. In other words, a zero. No other method of expressing quantity had ever before done that. It was a significant advance, a true milestone in human communication.

Because the zero glyph conveys the concept of a void, there is usually a tendency to overlook the fact that it is the cornerstone of modern mathematics. For the mark we toss off so lightly as a "zip" and a "goose egg" is what makes our numbers work so well. The truth is that the zero does double duty—it represents a void and also enables us to position our other number glyphs to alter their values. The symbol we use for two means a specific quantity to us when it stands alone: 2. But if that two moves one position to the left by the insertion of a zero after it, the quantity it represents increases ten times: 20. Add another zero to move it an additional position to the left and the quantity increases another ten times: 200. Suppose the quantity to be indicated is two hundred and two. By using a zero to show the position of each of the twos the solution is simplicity itself: 202. Thus, the remarkably effective role of the zero is to express a void and to serve as a positioner for other numbers. It is undeniable that the "nothing" symbol is the something that permits concise and precise expression of any number however large.

The system is so clearly superior to anything that went before it that one would suppose its spread from India to the rest of the world was rapid. Not so. Although Indian merchants following the trade routes westward carried with them word of the Hindu method of expressing quantity, it was not until the ninth century that it gained its first adherents abroad—in Baghdad on the Gulf of Arabia. From Baghdad Arabian traders carried the system farther westward to Europe where it was dismissed as a product of pagans and therefore unworthy. It was not until the fifteenth century that good sense overcame stupid prejudice and the Hindu-Arabic numbering system was adopted throughout Europe. European merchants, explorers, seamen, and soldiers spread the Hindu-Arabic system to the rest of the world.

Interestingly, although Hindu-Arabic numbers have become the world standard, Roman symbols still persist in use for certain purposes. It is the Roman numerals that are used to designate enthroned royalty from Queen Elizabeth II of England to King Sobhuza II of Swaziland to King Taufaahau Tupou IV of Tonga. Many tradition-conscious institutions also turn to this heritage from Rome for such ceremonial purposes as dating cornerstones and often for dating college diplomas.

Because royal and institutional allegiance to the Roman symbols is seen in many quarters as surrounding them with an air of grandeur, some canny businessmen adopt them for their products in the hope some of the prestige will rub off. Ford Motors does it with the Continental Mark V, professional football does it in the way it numbers the Super-bowls, the Cartier jewelry firm does it on the faces of its more expensive watches. However, there does not seem to be any particular reason why Hollywood studios almost always use Roman numerals to mark the copyright year of the films they produce, or why publishers of multivolume works usually turn to the Romans in numbering each volume.

Sometimes it does make sense to use Roman symbols in conjunction with the Hindu-Arabic glyphs in a numerical sequence that might otherwise become confusing. A Bible reference such as Proverbs V:19, or a theatrical reference such as Act I, Scene 6, gains clarity through the side-by-side employment of both systems.

The glyphs we lean on heavily for communicating quantitative information have become so much a part of the fabric of daily life that we even use them to convey unmathematical meanings. Tell someone you are going to pop into the "7-11" and he understands at once that you are going to a convenience food store. Tell him you are going to the "5 and 10" and he knows you are headed for the kind of store F. W. Woolworth popularized. Tell him you want to play "21" and he'll start to deal the cards. Tell him your girl-friend is "36-24-36" and he will envy you. If you see "57" on a bottle of catsup you know the tomatoes were processed by H. J. Heinz. If you come to a "30" on a manuscript you know you have reached the end of the text. And if you read that a friend got in the way of a "45" you go out to buy a card of condolence.

Experts agree on the qualities that make the most effective symbols. They are clear-cut and unambiguous. They are readily understood by the viewer regardless of his native tongue or his cultural background. They are distinctive in appearance so that recognition value is high. They are simple and uncluttered so that they can be reproduced easily.

While experts agree on what makes an effective symbol, they disagree on the form it should take. One group places emphasis on pictographs that present situations and objects with realism. Others favor glyphs that are merely suggestive of the situation or object, or completely arbitrary glyphs that are not at all suggestive of what they are intended to represent. Each group marshals arguments to bolster its case.

Those urging the use of realistic pictographs point out that they are more natural, direct, and easily learned because they bear a resemblance to what they stand for. Those who favor glyphs say the pictographers seem to present a strong case until you examine their reasoning closely. A pictograph valid today may become invalid tomorrow, they maintain. To prove their point they ask how many people still recognize an old-fashioned, rubber-bulb, automobile horn—a pictograph widely used abroad to indicate that horn-blowing is banned. These critics say the effectiveness of that pictograph ended when the old horn was outmoded and abandoned.

Even if progress does not cause a pictograph to become dated, its very realism can prove to be a handicap. Those who prefer glyphs cite a pictograph of an umbrella to support their claim. An umbrella is so clearly recognizable as exactly what it is that it ought not to be subject to misunderstanding, but it is not so. In the West a pictograph of an umbrella is a symbol for rain; in Africa it indicates royalty. Obviously what works in one situation may be completely unsuited to another.

Rudolf Modley, internationally respected symbologist told me: "Coming up with a symbol is no trick at all; any damn fool can do that. But creating a really good symbol, one that performs exactly as it is expected to, is quite another kettle of fish. That can be a maddeningly difficult task."

Modley's words have carried special weight among communicators since 1927 when—as a young, Austrian social scientist—he helped to develop the "Vienna method of pictorial statistics" to make complex data readily and universally understandable. In the Vienna system a housing chart, for instance, would use a rectangle with top bent like a peaked roof—easily recognizable as a symbolic house—to represent, say, 100 houses. Five such symbols, 500 houses. A faucet within a symbol: 100 houses with running water. Depict an electric light bulb beside the faucet and you understand at once that the 100 houses have electricity as well as running water. The opportunities to explain statistics concisely via the Vienna system are almost limitless.

For the last dozen years before his recent death, Modley and famed anthropologist Margaret Mead served as co-chairmen of Glyphs, Inc., a nonprofit organization functioning as an international clearing-house for research in symbology.

To illustrate the frustrating difficulties of creating a sound, foolproof symbol Modley recounted the episode of a carton of delicate, expensive laboratory equipment which was shipped to an Asiatic port: "The carton was conspicuously marked on all sides with a common pictograph for 'fragile,' a broken wineglass. The dockworker unloading the carton looked at the pictograph on it, shook his head in wonder over the crazy Westerners who ship broken glass abroad, and threw it onto a truck. As the carton hit the truckbed he could clearly hear broken glass rattling around."

Modley said there is only one way to avoid ending up with a symbol that boomerangs like the wineglass pictograph: "A team approach is needed, a coordinated effort by specialists in several fields: psychologists, sociologists, anthropologists, educators, administrators, and graphic designers. After the team agrees on a specific symbol, on the basis of each member's individual expertise, then it must evaluate the symbol in actual use under varied conditions and by varied groups. Only after all of the test results are in and modifications have been made in response to them should the symbol be adopted. It is an arduous process because there are no shortcuts and relying on guesswork or assumption is the way to end up with a carton of broken glass."

Dr. William L. Kelley, Georgetown University professor of psychology and coeditor of the *International Journal of Symbology*, is a firm believer that less is more where symbols are concerned, that the simpler and less complicated the glyph the more successfully it delivers its message.

"It is self-defeating to make symbols complex and intricate," he said. "Overdesigning simply leads to under-communicating. The emphasis has to be in the other direction, toward restrained, straightforward symbols. Consider what McDonald's does with only two golden arches. Regardless of what language you speak or what city, state, or country you are in, as soon as you see those arches you understand at once the composition of the menu, the price range, the character of the service, and the atmosphere of the establishment. That simple abstract glyph conveys a vast amount of information, and it does so quickly and clearly. Anyone seeking to capitalize intelligently on the potential of symbols as a means of effective communication needs to keep the example of the McDonald arches squarely in mind."

5

Expanding the Horizon

"But where is the 'john'?"

—Rudolf Modley

There is marked inconsistency in the way symbols are being put to work throughout the world today. From Toledo to Timbuktu glyphs and pictographs are adopted enthusiastically by special groups for special purposes. Yet, paradoxically, symbols are skimped as a unique channel for communication in the interest of the entire public.

In the words of one expert, "All around the globe there is an orientation toward limited-purpose, 'professional' glyphs—glyphs that are taught professionally, used professionally, and confined to relatively small groups. At the same time, there is a seeming inability to grasp the urgency of the need to put symbols to work intelligently for the larger needs of the general public. That makes as much sense as using medicines to treat only certain diseases instead of applying them to the whole range of illnesses they are capable of curing."

It's a good point. We have become a symbolized world, but primarily for narrow, limited purposes. Symbols enable practitioners of a vast number of human occupations to "talk shop" among themselves without resorting to conventional languages. Symbols convey a sense of national identity—the shamrock for the Irish, the maple leaf for the Canadians, the kangaroo for the Australians, wooden shoes for the Dutch. They convey a religious identity—the Cross of Christianity, the Star of David of Judaism, the Star and Crescent of Islam; or a political identity—the Democratic donkey, the Republican elephant, the hammer and sickle of communism, the clenched fist of the civil rights movement; or of corporate identity—the Amtrak arrow, the Pillsbury "doughboy," Prudential's "rock," PanAm's globe.

Symbols identify the things we are urged to buy, try, eat, drink, wear, use, visit, support, believe. On every side—from billboards, newspapers, pylons, television screens, in black-and-white and color and blinking lights—symbols assault everyone on behalf of goods, services, and concepts the modern world generates. Even emotions and abstractions have become symbolized—entwined hearts for love, Xs at the end of a letter for kisses, a halo for saintliness, a dove for peace.

Despite the bewildering variety that separates all these symbols, however, there is one characteristic that links them. They were conceived to serve the interests of the agency or group behind the symbol. Seldom are comparable levels of effort and resources devoted to creation of symbols for the sole, selfless purpose of serving the broad, general interests of the public at large.

As Rudolf Modley put it, "It has gotten so that you can't take a step without tripping over a glyph or a pictograph created for the benefit of whoever put the symbol there. Meanwhile, the ordinary citizen in the everyday kind of situation involving consumerism, safety, health, traffic, or recreation gets shortchanged on the symbols he needs. The public well-being demands a method of quick, clear communication through the fog of tongues and cultures blanketing the globe, and the evidence that symbols can provide that method is overwhelming. Yet little is being done about it and often the little that is done is done poorly. This is a ridiculous state of affairs that we can no longer afford to ignore. We have to do better with our so-called public symbols because the penalty we all pay for failure and delay has become intolerable. It is taking too much out of our hides."

Peering intently through his steel-rimmed glasses, words flavored by his native Viennese accent, Modley said wryly, "Take something as basic and as universally common to society as a public toilet, a facility you want to find in a hurry when you need it. Forget all the nonsensical verbal evasions like 'rest room,' 'powder room,' and 'lounge'; just consider the equally silly symbols that are invariably used—always a stylized silhouette wearing a skirt and one wearing pants and never a 'john' depicted although that is the whole purpose of the exercise. In many places, India and Scotland among them, men often wear skirts and almost everywhere women wear pants much of the time. The result is that the symbols not only hide the room's real function but they also make it possible to confuse the identity of those for whom the room is intended. So the poor traveler venturing into strange territory in this multilingual world of ours has a tough time finding a place to respond when nature calls."

Public symbols were not always as evasive or as confusing as the toilet symbol that Modley cites. In medieval Europe, where illiteracy as well as a multiplicity of languages made communication a burden, there were directness and clarity in the public symbols adopted to cope with the problem. Identifying a shoemaker was easy: you looked for a sign with a boot on it. For a beer you watched for the sign with a tankard. Nobody missed the message of the barber pole, or the apothecary's mortar and pestle, or the loaves painted on the baker's sign, or the three gold balls of the pawnshop. But somewhere along the way from then until now the needs of the mass of people became overlooked.

What went wrong? If symbols have been around for so many centuries, and if professional and technical groups are able to use them so adroitly for their own purposes, why are there such lackluster results today in putting them to work for the general public? Failure by many government officials at all levels to recognize the potential of symbols, unwillingness to be innovative, administrative red tape, and just plain bungling all play a role.

Rudolf Modley put the case in strong terms: "Chalk it up to stupidity, to petty jealousies, and to bureaucratic indifference and laziness. Let me use the Olympic Games as an illustration of the kind of thing I mean. Every four years the Olympics draw millions of visitors from every corner of the globe. To prevent utter chaos, the local officials use a battery of glyphs and pictographs to give the hordes of visitors the information they must have, things like where to find a doctor or change money or rent a car or mail a letter, and how to recover lost luggage or travel from point A to point B. Regardless of how well those symbolized signs do their job the host country for the next Olympics caters to its own nationalistic ego by devising its own set of glyphs and pictographs. So everyone has to start all over again with a new batch of symbols that may not even be as good as the last ones.

"Or take the case of traffic signals. Everyone knows that 'stop' is a red disk and 'go' is a green disk. But everyone also knows that there is such a thing as color blindness; in fact, something like six persons out of every hundred suffer from defective color perception. So why in the name of common sense do both symbols have to be round? Why can't the green disk be a green triangle instead, with the 'stop' remaining as it is? That way, regardless of color vision, everyone would know what the traffic lights are trying to tell him."

Observers agree the public has been penalized by the failure of authorities to adopt a sound, comprehensive symbol system for general use. One of these experts, William R. Myers of the U.S. Department of Transportation, has been trying to do something about it since 1959. He has staked out for his concentrated attention the overwhelming jumble of signs confronting and confusing travelers in transportation complexes and in popular tourist centers.

In 1973, responding to a Myers proposal, the Secretary of Transportation established the Advisory Committee of Transportation-Related Signs and Symbols, with Myers as executive director and graphics designer Thomas H. Geismar as chairman. The committee commenced its work by gathering together twenty-four of the most used symbol systems from around the world and subjecting each to intensive analysis. From this detailed study came an appreciation of the strengths and weaknesses of each. This in turn enabled the committee to winnow out the strongest, most effective symbols among the various systems. Where none of the glyphs seemed precisely right, the committee chose the most likely candidate and modified it to attain greater effectiveness. In late 1974 the committee unveiled its first thirty-four approved symbols, with an additional thirty nearing final stages of completion.

The symbols are now in use in Boston, New York, Philadelphia, Washington, Williamsburg, and in parts of Florida and New Jersey. Reaction to them is being monitored closely to determine what, if any, further modification may be required. Then, after a five-year test period to establish the validity of the system, the Department of Transportation plans to propose it for standardized, worldwide adoption.

Many of the symbols, like a knife and fork for a restaurant, offer no surprises. But some are puzzling at first glance. One is sometimes mistaken for a television set although it is actually a head-on symbolization of a train and is intended to lead travelers to rail facilities. Another—portraying a pipe, a book, and a gift-wrapped box—is a sign for shops. Among tongue-in-cheek complaints that Myers reports receiving about the symbol is it ignores "booze and butts, the two biggest sellers of the duty-free shops." The toilet symbol does what Modley condemns by displaying the usual silhouette but no toilet.

The committee's biggest headache comes from the pictograph for "Hotel Information"—a figure lying in bed with a question mark encircled above it. "That one needs more work," Myers admits. "As it stands now it can mean too many things including where can I find a bed mate."

Although industry has been slow to take advantage of the capability of symbols to improve communications with consumers of its products, there has recently been a quickening movement. The late Henry Dreyfuss provided a significant push in the early 1960s. An innovative thinker and superb industrial designer, Dreyfuss persuaded Deere & Company, a giant among manufacturers of farm equipment, to let him create symbols for its agricultural machinery. For years he had been touting the advantages of symbols; now that he had his opportunity to prove his assertion he warmed to the task with enthusiasm. By the time he had finished he had designed a virtual vocabulary of glyphs to explain the purpose and method of operation of each lever and switch, the meaning of every dial and gauge, and the proper way to service and maintain the equipment.

The benefits were immediately apparent. With a single glyph, Deere was able to get across a message that previously had required a lengthy verbal explanation. The glyph was able to do so clearly regardless of the literacy or native tongue of the one who looked at it. For the farmer-consumer it meant safer, more effective, more confident use of his equipment, less out-of-service "downtime," and an end to such verbal challenges as "rotate lower cam-shaft locking device in a counter-clockwise direction." For the manufacturer it meant improvement in customer satisfaction (which translated itself into increased sales) and a dramatic shrinkage of the thick, costly instruction manuals which used to be published in the various languages of importing countries.

Because the results were so positive and readily applicable on an international basis, Deere placed its Dreyfuss glyphs in the public domain to make them freely available to everyone. They were later adopted as the industry standard by the American Society of Agricultural Engineers.

Other industries sat up and took note of what was happening down on the farm. Recognizing that what would work in agriculture would also work in other areas, a number of companies in fields as varied as sewing machines, computers, cameras, automobiles, and telephones commenced using glyphs and pictographs for many of their consumer products.

But industry and commerce have not yet fully grasped the potential of communication via symbols, so their move into symbolization has been erratic and spotty. Even when they have turned to symbols, they have not always done so as well as they might have.

The health industry, for instance, has often been less than brilliant in labeling its consumer medicines. Consider the matter of substances restricted to external application because they act as poisons if ingested into the body. The glyph for poison in the United States is a skull and crossbones, but in many foreign countries poison is often indicated by a snake. This inconsistency presents an obvious, built-in hazard for travelers who are familiar with one symbol but not the other. Even within the United States the familiar skull and crossbones can bring grief to American families because young children associate it with pirates and adventure and so, attracted by the glyph instead of repelled by it, they often end up swallowing poison.

Concern over this sad situation prompted the University of Pittsburgh's Children's Hospital to test a completely new glyph for poison—"Mr. Yuk." Indeed "yukky looking," Mr. Yuk is a sickly green face with tongue sticking out. After switching from the skull and crossbones to Mr. Yuk, Children's Hospital noted a marked decrease in instances of child poisoning. Encouraged by this success, authorities in other areas are starting to "yukify" their labels.

The public symbols that receive closest attention are undoubtedly related to highways and traffic. We are all either motorists or at the mercy of them, so we have a personal stake in how well traffic-related signs do their job. The usual opinion, confirmed in repeated polls, is that they do their job poorly. Major complaints include signs too perplexing to permit ready understanding; signs clustered together competitively so that their multiple messages become blurred into mass gibberish; and lack of uniformity from one place to another, with resulting confusion.

Authorities have been painfully slow in using symbols to help reduce the mayhem of the highways. Take, for example, a pedestrian crossing. There should be a single, effective way to mark crossings so that those on foot and those behind the wheel would get the message instantly, unmistakably.

But this is not so. In some places street crossings are indicated by a band of white bars painted over the roadway, in some places by a band of diagonals, and in other places by two parallel stripes reaching from curb to curb. Sometimes they are indicated by a pictograph of an adult walking, sometimes by a pictograph of two adult walkers, sometimes by a pictograph of an adult and child walking together, sometimes by two children, and sometimes by a child alone. And there is still another device often adopted by the authorities—an absurd sign reading: "PED XING." No rational being would assume that this chaotic situation serves the public interest. (In Saudi Arabia the standard pedestrian-crossing sign is a pictograph of a headless walker. Why headless? Because the Moslem faith does not approve depictions of the human image. Saudi traffic engineers get around the ban by leaving the head off the figure in their pictograph.)

Those responsible for public-service signs too often depend on words when a symbol—well-conceived and well-executed—could serve the need better. For example, one popular way the authorities compound the absurdity of "PED XING" is by expanding it to "NO PED

XING." Another popular ploy is to post a "No Jaywalking" sign. This has prompted many a confused visitor encountering it for the first time to wonder why a jay would rather walk than fly and how, in any event, the authorities could expect a jay to read a sign.

Too many officials seem not to have discovered that "word thinking" is a much more ponderous, complex process than "symbol thinking." They suppose, first of all, that the viewer is literate and then, if he is, that his literacy is in the language of the sign. Assuming that these conditions are met, then the viewer must read the words, comprehend their meaning, and decide what action on his part appears to be most consistent with the message on the sign. An intelligently symbolized sign cuts through these complexities. It does not require a touch of genius to perceive that a simple straight-ahead arrow on a sign is far preferable to one reading: "No turns permitted from this intersection."

And what is the meaning of "Speed Zone," a sign that pops up frequently on American roads? Does it mean you are at liberty to speed if you wish to? Or does it mean that you are prohibited from speeding? The words do not give the slightest clue concerning which of the two completely opposite meanings is intended.

Europe is far ahead of the United States in the use of traffic-related symbols. For dozens of years European countries—as well as many other nations around the world—have used uniform international roadsigns bearing standardized pictographs and glyphs. They are not all so well conceived that none can stand improvement, but they are a long step in the right direction. The important thing is that the system is in place, and despite its shortcomings, it works.

The lessons to be learned from the European plan finally percolated into the consciousness of the U.S. Congress when it passed the Highway Safety Act of 1973. In this law requiring the states to abide by specific standards in road construction and maintenance, one section provided for the posting of the international symbols.

Effects of the law are now being felt around the country, with a benefit to the public at large. However, many knowledgeable critics charge that the law is not accomplishing all it should because the states are slow to comply with its provisions. And federal authorities, playing politics, are reluctant to pressure the states to move faster.

Spokesmen for the National Highway Safety Administration grant that the pace is slow. "As far as road signs are concerned," one told me, "the rate of the changeover to the international symbols is based on the rate of the wear-out of the existing signs. Wear-out can take a long time, so replacement can take a long time." He also acknowledged that the act applies only to those highways which are supported by federal funding. So adoption of the international symbols may never come at all for the many thousands of miles of American roads which are funded locally.

The sluggish rate at which conversion to the international symbols is taking place across the nation is only one of the concerns of the symbologists. Another is that highway authorities who adopt the signs seem to accept them as being the ultimate answer and so are not committed to an effort to improve upon them. The symbols are good, but they are not *that* good. Surveys have shown that many viewers are prone to confuse the "Crossroads" glyph with the "First Aid" glyph, since both are crosses.

A study conducted among motorists in London revealed that only 37 percent of those polled understood the message of the symbol for "All Motor Vehicles Prohibited" and only 65 percent understood what the "No Passing" glyph was trying to tell them. In a second study conducted in Great Britain investigators found that about half of the drivers surveyed thought that the symbol for "Falling Rocks" meant to beware of rocks that *had* fallen while the other half thought it meant to beware of rocks that *might* fall. The distinction is important. Those who thought the warning related to rocks that had already fallen said they would probably look down at the road and decelerate to avoid colliding with the rocks. But those who thought the warning concerned rocks that might fall said they would look upward and accelerate to get out of the danger area quickly. Studies in other European countries confirm the belief that the international road symbols can be improved to serve the needs of the public better.

Most symbologists are realists who acknowledge that many of the public glyphs in use around the world today are—like the symbol for "Falling Rocks"—in need of improvement, or in some extreme cases, in need of scrapping entirely to permit a fresh start. They readily list the challenges confronting them.

One of the most vexing of these challenges is the creation of a better way to indicate "you must not." The most usual current method to inform a viewer symbolically that he must not do something—that a specific action or thing is banned—is to display the glyph for the thing that is banned and then to superimpose over it either a diagonal, red bar, or a black X. Critics point out that the viewer may not understand what is meant, by the bar or the X. Or he may catch such a hasty glimpse of the sign—as in the case of a speeding motorist—that the prohibition indicator does not register with him. In any event, they say, it is poor psychology to try to prevent something by displaying the very thing you seek to prevent. The other side to this coin is the challenge of devising a foolproof glyph for "you must" to get across the message that something is not merely permitted but is mandatory.

In addition to freely admitting that much remains to be achieved in the field of public symbols, most experts warn against trying to put all of the public's eggs into a symbol basket. They point out that a glyph is not always the best solution to a communications problem and that the number of public symbols adopted should be limited to those for which there is a substantial, demonstrated need.

According to Rudolf Modley, "It is a mistake to think that everything can be communicated by glyphs. For one thing, symbols must be learned—think how long it takes to learn the punctuation marks—and the less to learn and assimilate the better. For another thing, you don't need an overwhelmingly tremendous number to do the job right. Look what Shakespeare was able to do with just the 26 symbols of the alphabet."

But if many symbologists counsel restraint, there are some who take a completely opposite view, arguing that there are absolutely no limits to communication via symbols. They press for adoption of a full-fledged, universal language composed solely of symbols. They point to China and Japan, whose languages are written entirely in glyphs, and insist that what can work for the Chinese and Japanese can work for anyone. They ignore the fact that attaining a high degree of proficiency in writing either Chinese or Japanese is so inordinately difficult and time-consuming that even natives of those countries are comfortable with only a relatively small number of the thousands of characters confronting them.

One of the most convinced and energetic of all who believe that glyphs are the stuff of which an international language must be made is Charles K. Bliss of Australia. Now in his eighties, he traces his obsession with symbols back to his days as a schoolboy when he discovered that everywhere in the world H₂O means water. He was fascinated by the magic whereby it eliminated the need to understand *agua, voda, wasser, vattnet, apa, l'eau*, or any of the hundreds of other words that all mean water. He has never lost his awe of the power of symbols to communicate across linguistic and cultural barriers.

Bliss has created what is probably the most sophisticated of the half-dozen or so symbol languages that have emerged in the past quarter-century. His system is built around a small number of basic glyphs, only some one hundred in all. But the key lies in his imaginative technique whereby two or more of the glyphs can be combined to alter and amplify the meanings of the basic symbols. For instance, "man" is represented by λ and "music" by δ . To indicate a musician one combines the "man" and "music" glyphs to come up with $\lambda\delta$. If the musician happens to be female rather than male one simply substitutes the "woman" glyph for the "man" glyph and ends up with $\lambda\delta$. To indicate a concert hall, one combines three glyphs— Δ for "building," $?$ for "ear" or "to hear," and   for "music," producing $\Delta?\delta$.

Using the Bliss system it is technically possible to convey an understanding of virtually anything, including emotions and other abstract concepts. But in order to do so one must first devote an enormous amount of time and study to the system and must school himself to think in the special kind of logic and analysis that the technique demands. Even then the message cannot get through unless the person on the receiving end has gone through the same laborious process to learn the system. Perhaps the best indication of what is involved is the fact that when the inventor published a book to explain how his symbol system works he had to use 882 pages in which to do it.

It seems likely that a full-scale symbol language will never become more than a sophisticated parlor game with little, if any, practical application. But the very fact that a handful of innovative symbologists have been able to construct complete, graphic languages is not without potential benefit to us all. It demonstrates the possibilities that exist to systematize and improve our public symbols so that they communicate with the clarity and effectiveness required.

Symbologists worry that even after all of the research and development to produce public symbols that function with solid reliability, we still may be no better off. There is no requirement, either in the United States alone or in the world as a whole, that any of the symbols must be used. There exists no central authority, nationally or internationally, to establish standards for public symbols, to insure that the standards are fully adhered to, and then to mandate the use of approved public symbols.

Bill Myers, who is so optimistic over the travel-related glyphs that his Department of Transportation committee is now testing in tourist centers around the country, says, "We have had the most talented minds collaborating on these glyphs and we are now in the midst of a long, thorough test to prove them out. But in the end, after we have a tested, proven set of public symbols, nobody *has* to use them, not even other federal agencies. However, unless they are used in the widest possible way the whole thing becomes an exercise in futility and the public receives no benefit. The only solution is mandatory legislation to put symbols to work in the public interest."

Rudolf Modley put it this way: "The immediate, short-range need is for congressional legislation leading to a system of standardized, effective public symbols and requiring use of that system once it is approved and adopted. The longer-range need is for an international body, probably under the umbrella of the United Nations, to do the same thing on a worldwide basis. That is the only way to eliminate conflict and confusion, and to insure that public symbology achieves full maturity as a universally intelligible communicator for everyone everywhere."

6

The Colorful Communication

The tissue of the life to be
We weave with colors all our own.

—John Greenleaf Whittier

People have often turned to visual techniques in devising ways to communicate with others. Gestures and symbols are only a part of the story. Another part was revealed when Troy fell to a Greek army in 1184 B.C.

The Greeks had long laid siege to Troy. Finally, after heroic resistance, the defenses cracked when the invading force used the Trojan Horse subterfuge to infiltrate its soldiers into the city. Almost before the last of the defenders had been subdued, Queen Clytemnestra in distant Argos was made aware of the victory that her army had achieved. She received the news so swiftly because her army commander had had the foresight to erect a chain of watchtowers on peaks stretching back from the battlefield to her palace 500 miles away. As soon as he was certain that the besieged city was his, he put the torch to a signal fire in the first of his towers. Each succeeding tower touched off its own signal fire the instant it glimpsed the glow of the preceding tower and the message sped to Queen Clytemnestra on the chain of flames.

In the thirteenth century the Sultan of Egypt, fearing that the Mongol hordes in Persia were planning a lunge across the Euphrates River with Cairo as their ultimate target, took the precaution of building watchtowers along the thousand-mile route from Persia to the Egyptian capital. When the Mongols did, in fact, launch the anticipated attack the towers relaying the warning via their signal fires sped word from the Euphrates to Cario in less than eight hours. Warned so swiftly, the Sultan had ample time to marshal his forces, and he dealt the invaders a crushing blow.

In 1588 watchtower fires flashed news of the coming of the Spanish Armada from Plymouth, England, to London—a distance of 200 miles—in less than twenty minutes. Even today's telephone operators in Plymouth, coping with overloaded circuits and all the other gremlins that bedevil modern electronics, sometimes can't get a call through to London as rapidly as that.

While watchtower signal fires were an effective way to speed a message over a great distance, the system had two obvious limitations. The first drawback was that there was no flexibility in the technique; the message said only what had been agreed in advance would be the meaning of the fire: that the attack had begun, that the city had been captured, or whatever. The second drawback was that there had to be a direct line of sight between the receiver and the fire. It took the American Indian to figure out how to increase the range and flexibility of the signal fire.

74

The Indians fed damp grass and green vegetation to their fires to create thick plumes of smoke; it was the smoke, rather than the fire itself, which they used for communication. The smoke rose high in the air, carried aloft by the updraft of heat from the fire. Under favorable conditions it could be seen for fifty miles and more.

The smoke itself was controlled by alternately covering and uncovering the fire with an animal hide or blanket. The way in which the covering was manipulated governed the smoke puffs that were released—their number, length, patterns—enabling the Indians to transmit messages that were infinitely more informative than those of a simple fire alone. Often they achieved even greater flexibility by employing as many as four smoke fires simultaneously. Others also used smoke signals—the Chinese, the aborigines of Australia, the Maoris of New Zealand—but none used it quite so well as the American Indian. In fact, nobody improved on the Indian's mastery of the smoke signal until well into this century when imaginative advertisers teamed up with barnstorming aviators to come up with skywriting by airplanes.

While the Indian smoke signal was flourishing, a technique for visual communication came into prominence: mirrors to reflect the rays of the sun in a coded sequence. Actually, it was not really new. Archimedes had used mirrors to send out messages during the battle for Syracuse in the third century B.C. But it had fallen into disuse. The British army breathed fresh life into the technique when it devised the heliograph during the campaigns in India in the 1800s.

The heliograph was a signaling mirror with an arrangement of movable shutters fixed in front of it. Alternately opening and closing the shutters enabled the sender to control the duration of the reflected flashes with an ease and a precision that made the transmission of complex coded messages a simple matter. The heliograph is still sometimes used today for communication between vessels at sea, especially between military vessels that wish to maintain radio silence for tactical reasons.

But of all of the ways to convey information visually one of the most subtle and enduring is the method created by Theseus, hero of ancient Greek mythology.

We recall Theseus for his legendary foray against the Minotaur, the monster that exacted an annual sacrifice of seven Athenian youths and seven Athenian maidens. Resolved to slay the bloodthirsty monster, Theseus persuaded his father, King Aegeus, to let him sail to Crete and challenge the Minotaur in its lair. Before he left Athens, Theseus devised a way to hasten word of the outcome to his anxious father. He promised that if he were successful he would raise white sails on his vessel for its return voyage; if the Minotaur prevailed, the crew would return under the black sails that the craft customarily used. The color code would enable lookouts posted on the coastal heights to bring King Aegeus word of the result while the boat was still at a distance from Athens.

Theseus did go to Crete, engaged the Minotaur in mortal combat, and slew it. On the return voyage, however, he forgot to substitute white sails for the normal black ones. The waiting lookouts, glimpsing the black sails of the approaching vessel, rushed word to the King that Theseus had been slain. King Aegeus was so distraught by the assumed death of his son that he leaped into the sea and drowned himself.

The legend does more than simply demonstrate that Theseus was very much better at swordsmanship than at remembering. It also illustrates the fact that color constitutes a means of visual communication.

All of us receive color messages that often have the capacity to stir us deeply. Red, white, and blue arouse our pride and patriotism. We become solemn when we receive the mournful message of a black armband. We see the purple mantle of royalty and feel the presence of the sovereign.

Colors are so communicative that we have even developed a tendency to inject them into our speech. We say we are in the pink when we are feeling good, in the black when affluent, blue when depressed, yellow when cowardly. We become green with envy and white with rage. If we are optimists we are looking through rose-colored glasses, and if embarrassed we turn crimson. A choice investment is gilt-edged. If our plants thrive it is because we have a green thumb. Aristocrats are blue bloods and puritanical laws are blue laws. Extortion is blackmail and a cover-up is a whitewash.

But color has to be handled with a knowing touch; if mishandled, it can deliver a faulty message, like the one to King Aegeus. The white that signals purity and innocence in the West is a sign of mourning among Koreans and Chinese, but the black that is an indication of mourning in the West is a sign of good fortune among Ethiopian tribesmen.

Red can be especially tricky. In Russia it signifies beauty, in China it is the color for brides, and in much of Africa it is the color for funerals. In Japan, red is the chief color of the Shinto religion but in much of the rest of the world it indicates immoral activities and is used to mark off "red light" districts. In Morocco, homosexuals wear red shirts to signal that they are gay. Among most Italians the yolk of an egg is the "red," but while an American with an empty pocketbook is "in the red" the Italian who is broke is "in the green."

Red can even be confusing in such an unexpected field as public safety. By international agreement red is accepted around the world to signal danger. It follows then that a factory using a bucket to contain an inflammable liquid would customarily paint the bucket red. But what color should a factory use for a fire bucket containing water? Again the bucket is almost always red because red is the traditional color for fire engines and other defenses against fires. So red can be both a hazard and a protection in normal industrial usage. A technician in a Virginia plant was victimized by this conflict when he tried to quench a glowing welding rod in a red bucket that he assumed held water for protection against fire. The bucket actually contained a volatile solvent, and the resulting explosion killed the unfortunate welder.

Highway engineers everywhere use red and green for traffic lights because everyone understands that red means stop (danger) and green means go (safety). But what color should be used to mark an emergency exit? Should it be red because it leads away from danger, or should it be green because it leads to safety? There is as much logic behind one choice as the other. In most of the United States the "away from danger" point of view prevails, and so most American exits are indicated in red. But in some western states and some foreign countries the "to safety" outlook prevails, and in those places emergency exits are marked in green. For travelers passing through strange territory the distinction can make a crucial difference.

There is no such confusion in the use of color for communication among mariners. For centuries colored signal flags have delivered messages back and forth clearly and quickly between ships on all of the world's waterways. Depending upon its color and design, each flag stands for a different letter of the alphabet. But to spell out a message letter by letter would be a tedious process and would require both the sender and the receiver to spell it out in a tongue that they both shared. The beauty of the maritime signal flag system is that it eliminates both of these hindrances.

Suppose, for example, that the captain of an American vessel wishes to inform the captain of a Brazilian vessel: "I have received serious damage in collision." The American *could* employ 37 different flags, one for each of the letters in his message, hoping that the Brazilian would understand the English-language words they spelled out. But under the internationally adopted system the American skipper merely hoists two flags: the first a yellow rectangle with a black ball in its center, the second a white rectangle containing a blue cross. The first flag represents the letter "I" and the second represents the letter "X." However, every mariner—whatever his native tongue may be—knows that the "IX" combination means "I have received serious damage in collision." And if he has forgotten what the combination means he need simply look it up in the signal book that vessels carry. Literally thousands of messages can be conveyed swiftly via specific combinations of maritime flags.

Colored flags have proven to be such efficient message bearers that their use has spread to fields far removed from the sea. There are few who would not immediately understand the "I surrender" meaning of a white flag or the "Medical attention available here" message of a white flag containing a red cross. Experienced antique hunters know that a red flag posted outside an auction house means "Auction is being held here today." For soldiers, on the other hand, the red flag delivers a different message; they know better than to wander out on the firing range when a red flag flies over it because that indicates a firing exercise is in progress. Every football fan understands that the yellow flag thrown onto the field by an official signifies a player has committed an infraction of the rules. And racing car buffs understand the color language of the track from the green flag signaling the start of the race to the blue flag signaling the last lap and the black-and-white flag for the finish.

One traditional use of color has been to combine it with a special design to create an insignia of identity. The custom dates back so far into the past that it is even mentioned by Homer in the epic poems he wrote earlier than 700 B.C. But heraldry, to give it its proper name, really commenced to flower in the twelfth century when it became a widespread custom among European noblemen to adopt personal coats of arms.

Colorful banners containing their distinguishing insignia became a commonplace sight to mark places under their control and troops under their command. The flags were especially useful amid the confusion of the battlefield to communicate locations of different forces quickly. The adoption of identifying flags and coats of arms is now firmly rooted everywhere—and for much more than simply denoting noble lineage. It identifies nations and other political jurisdictions, academic and cultural institutions, and associations and groups of every kind. It has even become a fixture in the business world where many corporations fly "house" flags to transmit a sense of their identity. Even the way in which a flag is displayed can convey information. Few would miss the message of mourning that is delivered by a flag flown at half-staff, or the message of distress delivered by a national flag flown in an inverted position.

Perhaps one of the most imaginative uses of color for communication was the one conceived by the Incas in what was later to become Peru. The Incas created the *quipu*, a highly sophisticated arrangement incorporating colored cords and knots. Each color had a specific meaning, such as green for grain, red for soldiers, white for silver, yellow for gold, and so on. The knots, too, had specific meanings, all of them related to quantities. Units of ten, for example, were represented by single knots, and units of a hundred by double knots. In addition, the pattern in which the colored cords were attached to one another conveyed a special meaning.

The Inca empire covered wide territory and embraced several subjugated tribes speaking various languages. Administering this empire, levying taxes, issuing military orders to outposts, and many other tasks all were troublesome because of the languages and distances involved and because the Incas themselves had no written language. That was why the *quipu* was developed. To send a message, one called on the local *quipucamayocuna,* "the keeper of the knots," and told him what was to be transmitted. He selected cords of the appropriate colors, tied the required number and types of knots in them in the appropriate places, and then fastened the colored, knotted cords to a central cord in a particular pattern. The whole thing was turned over to relay runners who sped it to its destination. Of course the *quipu* was so complicated that it could be read only by another *quipucamayocuna* at the destination. So runners were constantly speeding through the countryside carrying *quipu* back and forth among *quipucamayocunas* who were posted throughout the empire the way telegraph offices are located throughout the United States.

Somewhat similar to the *quipu,* though not nearly as sophisticated or complex, was a system adopted by tribes in parts of Africa and Asia. They employed wooden sticks with notches instead of knots and colors, embodying their messages in the number and design of the notches cut into the message-sticks. It was a useful way to send limited information on a few, specific matters.

7

Dots and Sniffs

One thing I know—that I am he
Who once was blind, and now I see.

—John Hay

Paris in 1824 was a depressing place, the focal point for political turmoil and social unrest that gripped France. With the concentration of the blind, Louis Braille listened to a friend read the morning newspaper to him. He found no comfort in the accounts of the nation's upheaval, but then his friend read a short, back-page item that excited Braille.

The brief account described a newly developed French Army procedure enabling front-line observers to write and read operational messages at night without using a light and thus risk discovery by the enemy. The new system was highly original. It completely eliminated conventional reading and writing, replacing them instead with communication by touch. There were two keys to the technique. First, the message was conveyed in a code consisting of geometric shapes instead of conventional words. (That is, a right angle might mean "enemy advancing on right flank," a left angle might mean "enemy advancing on left flank," a square might mean "no enemy movement observed," and so on.) The second key to the technique involved distinctive shapes pressed into soft paper with small, metal stamps which left raised impressions on the back of the sheet. To "write," one simply pressed the appropriate stamps into the message form. To "read," one simply passed a finger over the back of the form to identify the shapes of the impressions raised there by the stamps. The article concluded by reporting that the Ministry of the Army had conducted a test of the system and found it effective.

Louis Braille immediately grasped the significance of the technique. This, he was convinced, offered a clue to how the blind might read and write by touch.

A method of communication by touch had already been attempted in the small institute for the blind that Braille attended in Paris. But it was an overwhelmingly awkward process requiring a special press to emboss headline-sized letters into a page so that they formed very high ridges reproducing the shapes of the letters. The giant size and height of the ridges were necessary to permit distinguishing by touch alone between such quite similar shapes as "o" and "c" and "e," "m" and "n," "i" and "l," "h" and "b."

Because each embossed letter occupied so much space in three dimensions—length, width, and thickness—an ordinary book became a massive affair that had to be separated into some twenty sections, each a dozen times larger than an entire, conventionally printed book. The embossed books were so huge and so inordinately expensive to produce that the institute had succeeded in turning out a grand total of only a single copy of each of fourteen different books. Furthermore, the process did not address itself at all to the problem of enabling the blind to write, only—in its awkward, laborious fashion—to the problem of enabling the blind to read.

Braille was determined to find the means of adapting the military system to the much broader needs of civilian society. It turned out to be a long, challenging quest that led Braille to many frustrating dead ends. But each time that happened he started anew. Ultimately he was successful in creating a wholly effective, convenient method of communication for the blind.

The heart of Braille's system was a so-called "cell" consisting of a maximum of six dots. The number of dots used and their placement determined the meaning of each cell. In all, the cells provided the possibility of sixty-three different patterns, enough for all of the letters of the alphabet, the punctuation marks, the numbers from zero to nine, and a few of the most frequently used words. The system that Braille designed has since become the international language of the blind for reading, writing, musical notation, and mathematical and scientific computation. Amazingly, Louis Braille was only a teenager when he made his monumental breakthrough.

The way in which Braille is written today is very little changed from the original procedure. The writer inserts a sheet of paper between two metal plates. The upper plate is divided into rows of perforated, six-dot cells. The lower plate is divided into matching rows of six-dot indentations. The writer presses a stylus into the appropriate holes in the perforated cells in the upper plate and the stylus creates dimples in the paper by pushing it into the matching indentations in the lower plate. Braille can also be typed on a special typewriter. Those trained in

Braille are able to pass their fingertips swiftly over a page of dotted cells and absorb their meaning at a pace that compares favorably with that of a sighted person reading conventional printing. For the blind the sense of touch has become an effective substitute for the sense of sight.

But the sense of touch is also a useful channel for communication among the sighted. More often than one might imagine, we send and receive messages by touch. Our most common form of communication by touch— or tactile communication—is the handshake, which can express various messages. There are, among others, the firm grip that signals a genuine greeting, the "limp dishrag" touch that suggests indifference, the caressing clasp that sends a sexual message.

Patting has its own set of messages—the mother's calming pat to quiet a cranky infant, the shoulder pat that conveys sympathy, the hearty slap on the back that expresses approval, the pat on the fanny by which players congratulate a teammate who has just pulled off a sparkling play. The nudge—first cousin to the pat—also has its distinctive vocabulary, from the poke in the ribs to punctuate a joke, to the furtive nudge that suggests conspiracy, to the gentle nudge that counsels caution.

Tactile communication even plays a role in the realm of business and industry. The Federal Highway Administration is currently studying the way that touching can deliver information to improve the level of automotive safety. It is considering instructions to the automobile industry to engineer tactile communication into the control knobs the driver must use in operating his vehicle. Some manufacturers have already beaten the Federal Highway Administration to the punch. Honda, for instance, now makes its instrument panel controls in distinctive, individualized shapes that identify them clearly.

Thus, by touch alone, the driver can distinguish among the controls on the panel, picking out the lights, windshield wiper, and other functional knobs without taking his eyes away from the road. In some situations this kind of instant, foolproof communication could be a life-saver.

In a different commercial application of the sense of touch, Holland has begun printing its paper money with the addition of raised dots in the surface to identify value. While this innovation is intended to enable the blind to feel out the denomination of their bills, it has also been found useful to sighted persons in darkness. The dotted-money program has had such a favorable reception that Switzerland, taking note of the results, is now planning to follow suit with its own national currency.

The newest marketplace application of tactile communication has just been devised by a Pennsylvania State University research team investigating consumer safety. The Penn State development adds a new dimension to the consumer's defenses against hazardous packaged products by printing warning labels on paper that has been treated so that it has a rough, sandpaperlike surface. The idea is that if a container holding a dangerous product is picked up unknowingly the consumer will be alerted to his peril by the prickly warning he feels through his fingers.

How much tactile communication has become a part of our lives is revealed in our reactions to many situations. When we see something that moves us deeply, we unconsciously describe it in tactile terms by referring to it as a "touching" scene. If someone tries to borrow money from us he is "hitting us up for a touch." Someone who annoys us "rubs us the wrong way" or "gets under our skin." Someone who is easily persuaded to do something is a "soft touch." If we are quick to take offense we are "thin-skinned" and if we lack sensitivity we are "thick-skinned." We speak of conflicting pressures as the "rub."

One of the most underrated parts of the human body is the nose, which serves as a message center. Whether we realize it or not, we depend on our noses for a variety of information. The nose is amazingly sensitive. Helen Keller, though blind and deaf, could identify friends by the subtly different smell each emitted. Desert nomads of the Sahara can detect the odor of a campfire as far as twenty-five miles away. Albert Weber, a U.S. Food and Drug Administration chemist, is responsible for analyzing commercial foods of every description from canned chili to cod fish filets in order to grade them according to their suitability for human consumption. He can do in one minute of sniffing what would otherwise require at least a full day of complex chemical analysis in the laboratory, and he can do it with a degree of accuracy that is at least as reliable as the laboratory's. Weber is only one of several FDA "smellers" protecting the American public with their noses.

The business world has been quick to recognize the value of the nose as a communicator. The most obvious examples are perfumes, toiletries, deodorants. But they are only the tip of the nasal iceberg. Some commercial baking establishments add an artificial "fresh butter" odor to their products to enhance sales appeal. Used-car dealers spray the interiors of their automobiles with a "new car" smell to makes their clunkers seem to have just rolled off the assembly line. Carpet makers use floral scents to kill the unpleasant smell of dyes and materials used in their manufacture. Scores of ugly duckling household products from detergents to floor waxes have the odor of lemon or lime in order to deliver a more attractive message to the housewife.

But the nose is also used by business for the delivery of messages that have no direct link with the cash register.

Industrial plants which manufacture gas used for home heating mix a "gas odor" into their virtually odorless product as a safety device enabling the homeowner to quickly detect hazardous leaks in his system. When a dangerous condition develops in underground shafts, mine operators can alert the work crew to the peril by injecting a distinctive gas into the mine's ventilating ducts. The nasal message spreads quickly and clearly throughout the mine.

There is a significant communication role for the nose in the field of medicine. Doctors are often able to diagnose an illness on the basis of its tell-tale odor. In an emergency situation this identification of a disease by its smell signature can have a major impact on the future well-being of the patient. In fact, when medicine was a simpler science often diagnoses were made with remarkable accuracy of such diseases as scurvy, diphtheria, impetigo, yellow fever, typhoid fever, and plague on the basis of distinctive smells.

The nose has even been put to work on the battlefield. During World War I both the Allies and Germans often launched poison gas attacks which felled those who did not don their masks promptly. But those who did get them on in time found their movements and vision hampered. The offensive side was a frequent victim of its own chemical attack because shifting winds would waft the gases back on the attackers. To protect its soldiers from its own gases the U.S. Army put in butyl mercaptan, a penetrating, foul-smelling substance that was harmless itself but served as a quick, unmistakable warning a lethal chemical was loose. It did not take the Germans long to discover that the sign of an American attack was the stench of the butyl mercaptan. They issued strict orders that at the first whiff of it German troops must don their masks to protect against a coming attack. But the U.S. Army then made an adroit countermove by launching butyl mercaptan alone without any accompanying lethal gases. The Germans dutifully put their masks on, but the American soldiers, knowing that a wind shift could not expose them to anything worse than a terrible smell, did not hamper themselves with masks. Thus they were able to maneuver more freely and more effectively than their enemy.

A couple of wars later, the nose played a new role in combat when the U.S. Army introduced "people sniffers" to the Vietnam battlefield. These were ingenious, extremely sensitive devices able to pinpoint the location of enemy troops in dense jungle by detecting the faintly pungent message of the chemical salts that their bodies produce naturally.

The nose is even capable of communication on a cultural plane. Educators have found they can improve the reading ability of children by using special teaching cards which contain the word being taught plus the particular smell associated with it. The card for "garage," for instance, is impregnated with the oily, greasy odor that characterizes a garage; the card for "bacon" gives off the odor of frying bacon; the card for "lily" smells like lilies. Taking a slightly different approach, some museums now incorporate suitable scents into many of their exhibits to communicate a greater degree of realism to the viewers. Industrial displays smell like the industries they portray, a marine exhibit emits the odors of the sea, a replica of a cave dwelling smells musty and smoky, a blacksmith's shop smells of hot metal, harness, and horses.

But the versatility of communication by smell is demonstrated best, perhaps, by its enduring role in religious practice. Five thousand years ago the Egyptians worshipped Ra—their sun god—by burning incense in his honor, believing that its scent would reach him with a message of their devotion. The Greeks and the Romans employed a wide variety of perfumes and aromatic plant extracts to convey their spiritual messages. Fragrant sandalwood is associated with Hindu temples, and the delicate scent of musk is associated with Moslem mosques. Aromatic frankincense and myrrh are recorded in the Bible as gifts of the Magi. Both scents played a role in religious rites. Frankincense is, in fact, still used for that purpose and delivering its religious message.

8

The Last Word

As World War II drew to a close, the late Robert Maynard Hutchins, then chancellor of the University of Chicago, observed that "a world community can exist only with world communication, which means something more than extensive shortwave facilities scattered about the globe. It means common understanding."

Our excursion into human communication started out by venturing among words of conventional language where we discovered that words are not always reliable pathways to the common understanding Dr. Hutchins sought. We continued, exploring the means, other than conventional speech, whereby people can transmit their thoughts to others effectively. Our exploration has been lively because people turn out to be imaginative, resourceful, spirited communicators who find all sorts of ways to get their messages to others.

The limitations of conventional language which we have discussed should not obscure the great power words possess when used suitably. What is needed is a sense of balance. If there is to be an awareness of what words cannot do, there must also be a corresponding appreciation of what they are capable of. If there are situations in which words do not measure up to the need, there are those in which only words will suffice.

Without words we would be denied the brilliance and the grace of a Tennyson, a Molière, a Dante, or a George Bernard Shaw. We would be denied the inspiration of the Magna Charta, the Declaration of Independence, the Bill of Rights, the Gettysburg Address. Would Martin Luther King's "I have a dream," or Franklin D. Roosevelt's "All we have to fear is fear itself," or General Douglas MacArthur's "I shall return" have had the same impact if they had been delivered in symbols or in smoke signals? Or, for that matter, would Will Rogers and Jack Benny have provided us with so much good humor had there been no words?

Ultimately, we should recognize that people have created choices to satisfy the unquenchable human need to communicate with one another. Sometimes one option suits the circumstances best, sometimes another is the wisest choice. The important point is that, given half a chance, people find a way to communicate with one another. As long as there is communication there is hope for humanity. Dr. Hutchins' world community based on common understanding may yet come to pass.

Index

The Author

Vernon Pizer is the author of the popular *Ink, Ark., and All That: How American Places Got Their Names*, from Putnam's. A free-lance writer, based in Washington, D.C., he is the author of more than 300 articles in major publications and a half-dozen books. Mr. Pizer entered the Army in World War II, serving in North Africa and Europe, and retired from military service as a lieutenant colonel in 1963.